A FOOTHILLS MEADOW IN BLOOM

GLACIERS ON THE MINARETS

LE CONTE FALLS ON TUOLUMNE RIVER

A FIELD AT TIMBER LINE

SEQUOIAS IN CONGRESS GROVE

MIRROR LAKE

THE GREAT WESTERN DIVIDE FROM ABOVE THE MIDDLE FORK OF THE KAWEAH RIVER

Other Publications:

THE HIGH SIERRA

THE AMERICAN WILDERNESS / TIME-LIFE BOOKS / ALEXANDRIA, VIRGINIA

BY EZRA BOWEN

AND THE EDITORS OF TIME-LIFE BOOKS

Time-Life Books Inc.
is a wholly owned subsidiary of

TIME INCORPORATED

FOUNDER: Henry R. Luce 1898-1967

Editor-in-Chief: Henry Anatole Grunwald
President: J. Richard Munro
Chairman of the Board: Ralph P. Davidson
Executive Vice President: Clifford J. Grum
Chairman, Executive Committee: James R. Shepley
Editorial Director: Ralph Graves
Group Vice President, Books: Joan D. Manley
Vice Chairman: Arthur Temple

TIME-LIFE BOOKS INC.

MANAGING EDITOR: Jerry Korn
Text Editor: George Constable
Board of Editors: Dale M. Brown, George G. Daniels,
Thomas H. Flaherty Jr., Martin Mann, Philip W. Payne,
Gerry Schremp, Gerald Simons
Planning Director: Edward Brash
Art Director: Tom Suzuki
  Assistant: Arnold C. Holeywell
Director of Administration: David L. Harrison
Director of Operations: Gennaro C. Esposito
Director of Research: Carolyn L. Sackett
  Assistant: Phyllis K. Wise
Director of Photography: Dolores A. Littles

CHAIRMAN: John D. McSweeney
President: Carl G. Jaeger
Executive Vice Presidents: John Steven Maxwell,
David J. Walsh
Vice Presidents: George Artandi, Stephen L. Bair,
Peter G. Barnes, Nicholas Benton, John L. Canova,
Beatrice T. Dobie, Carol Flaumenhaft, James L. Mercer,
Herbert Sorkin, Paul R. Stewart

THE AMERICAN WILDERNESS

EDITOR: Charles Osborne
Editorial Staff for *The High Sierra*
Picture Editor: Susan Rayfield
Designer: Charles Mikolaycak
Staff Writer: Betsy Frankel
Chief Researcher: Martha T. Goolrick
Researchers: Terry Drucker, Margo Dryden,
Susanna Seymour, Timberlake Wertenbaker
Design Assistant: Mervyn Clay
Picture Coordinator: Joan Lynch

Revisions Staff
EDITOR: Rosalind Stubenberg
Chief Researcher: Barbara Levitt
Text Editors: Sarah Brash, Lee Greene
Researcher: Reiko Uyeshima
Copy Coordinator: Anne T. Connell
Art Assistant: Jeanne Potter
Editorial Assistants: Mary Kosak, Linda Yates

Editorial Operations
Production Director: Feliciano Madrid
  Assistants: Peter A. Inchauteguiz, Karen A. Meyerson
Copy Processing: Gordon E. Buck
Quality Control Director: Robert L. Young
  Assistant: James J. Cox
  Associates: Daniel J. McSweeney, Michael G. Wight
Art Coordinator: Anne B. Landry
Copy Room Director: Susan B. Galloway
  Assistants: Celia Beattie, Ricki Tarlow

The Author: A native of the East, Ezra Bowen has spent considerable time in the West—including the wilderness of the Sierra Nevada. Bowen began his writing career as a reporter for *Newsweek.* He later served for 10 years as a writer and senior editor for *Sports Illustrated.* He joined Time-Life Books as Director of Educational Research and Development in 1964, then resumed his writing in late 1965. Co-author of the LIFE Science Library's *Wheels,* he wrote the *Middle Atlantic States* volume of the TIME-LIFE Library of America and edited the Time-Life series This Fabulous Century and The Old West. He has been an assistant managing editor of Time-Life Books and editor-in-chief of American Heritage Books.

The Consultant: Martin Litton, who was born in California, made his first trip into the Sierra at 16—with one other boy and a donkey to carry their gear. Since then he has walked most of the high wild parts of the range. Following World War II service as an Army Air Force pilot, Litton wrote features about the outdoors for the *Los Angeles Times,* and later joined *Sunset* magazine. Since leaving the magazine in 1969, Litton, who is a past director of the Sierra Club, has been a freelance photographer and writer on the wilderness.

The Cover: One of a group of unnamed lakes at 11,000 feet in Upper Pioneer Basin (part of the John Muir Wilderness) reflects the setting sun. Mount Mills (13,468 feet) rises above the snow field at center, and Mount Abbot (13,715 feet) is at left.

CORRESPONDENTS: Elisabeth Kraemer (Bonn); Margot Hapgood,
Dorothy Bacon, Lesley Coleman (London); Susan Jonas, Lucy T.
Voulgaris (New York); Maria Vincenza Aloisi, Josephine du Brusle
(Paris); Ann Natanson (Rome). Valuable assistance was also
provided by: Carolyn T. Chubet, Miriam Hsia, Christina Lieberman
(New York); Mimi Murphy (Rome); Pat Tucker (Washington, D.C.).

For information about any Time-Life book, please write:
Reader Information
Time-Life Books
541 North Fairbanks Court
Chicago, Illinois 60611

Library of Congress Cataloguing in Publication Data
Bowen, Ezra.
  The high Sierra, by Ezra Bowen and the editors of Time-Life
Books. New York, Time-Life Books [1972]
  184 p. illus. (part col.) 27 cm. (The American wilderness)
Bibliography: p. 181.
  1. Sierra Nevada Mountains.   I. Time-Life Books.   II. Title.
F868.S5B6   917.94'4'045   78-179462
ISBN 0-8094-1139-3
ISBN 0-8094-1141-5 lib. bdg.
ISBN 0-8094-1140-7 retail ed.

TIME-LIFE is a trademark of Time Incorporated U.S.A.

Contents

1/ The Air the Angels Breathe 20

The Age of John Muir 34

2/ A Country Standing on End 48

The Sculptured Rock 64

3/ The Range of Light 72

A Continent on a Mountain 88

4/ Four Sierra Creatures 104

A Nature Walk along McGee Creek 124

5/ The Cabinet of Curiosities 136

Spring in the Sierra 146

6/ Preserving What Is Left 156

Discovery of a Living Valley 170

Acknowledgments and Bibliography 180

Credits 181

Index 182

The Setting of the Sierra

The Sierra Nevada region, covering an enormous section of California and a small corner of Nevada (shaded area at right), is mapped below, highlighting the features discussed in this book. The mountain terrain of the high Sierra appears in yellow, with surrounding foothills and lowlands shown in green. Red outlines enclose tracts of federally protected land: national parks, national forests, primitive areas and sections set aside permanently by the Wilderness Act of 1964. Lakes and rivers are portrayed in blue; lake beds that contain water only part of the year appear here as mottled blue areas surrounded by broken lines. Black triangles mark major peaks, round dots towns and cities. Squares denote points of scenic, recreational or historic interest. Otherwise, standard map symbols are used. Trails are shown by black lines, paved roads by double lines, railroads by lines with crossbars.

1/ The Air the Angels Breathe

*How deathlike is sleep in this mountain air, and quick
the awakening into...life! A calm dawn...then
floods of sun-gold, making everything tingle and glow.*

JOHN MUIR/ *MY FIRST SUMMER IN THE SIERRA*

On an Indian summer morning three horsemen turn a string of pack
mules onto a trail that climbs among the conifers and tumbled rocks at
the head of Cottonwood Canyon, high on the eastern rim of the Sierra
Nevada wilderness, about 260 miles southeast of San Francisco. The
October sun is hard and white; there is no cloud nor even a hint of
morning dew upon the air. Each thud of a hoof sends up a tiny explosion of rock dust to settle onto the leaves of trailside shrubs or to
sift upward into the nostrils and throats of the riders, who are breathing
deeply and thirstily in the unaccustomed thinness of the atmosphere
above 10,000 feet.

There was a light freeze along the trail here last night, and in a patch
of alpine meadow dampened by the seepage from Cottonwood Creek
the mud is puckered by frost boils. In one north-facing copse, where the
porous soil holds the hoofprints of mule deer, frost crystals gleam on the
sedge and shriveled ruins of shooting-star blossoms sag on their stems.
Ahead a fat marmot, already drowsy from the impulse to hibernate,
whistles its disapproval at the approaching horses, and then waddles
slowly into its rock burrow.

Somewhat like the marmot, the horsemen are adjusting to a change in
their environment; but to them the transition has been sudden and not a
little disorienting. Only two hours earlier they were 7,000 feet lower,
in the heavier air and desert heat of the Owens Valley—still in

sight to the east of the trail they are riding. The quick gain in altitude has left them feeling dehydrated, vaguely headachy and more enervated than they would like to be in the first hour of a week-long ride into the high country. Moreover the morning sun has not yet burned off the last of the night's chill, and the riders turn up the collars of sheepskin and canvas jackets as a wind comes tumbling down Cottonwood Canyon. Mark Twain, who roughed it through the Sierra much in the manner of these horse-borne campers, was himself often discommoded by the numbing drops in temperature bred by the mountain winds. "I have seen a perfectly blistering morning open up with the thermometer at ninety degrees at eight o'clock," he once commented, "and seen the snow fall fourteen inches deep.... There are only two seasons in the region . . . the breaking up of one winter and the beginning of the next . . . it snows at least once in every single month."

It still does. In the warm week before a recent Labor Day, a mother whose two youngsters were sleeping outdoors below timber line awoke to a commotion outside her cabin. She looked out onto ground covered by new snow; the kids were shouting, groaning, shaking the snow off their sleeping bags and trying to slap and finger-comb the matted ice from their hair. In July of 1941 at old Army Pass, just around an ice-cracked cliff from the Cottonwood trail, a party of hikers spent an hour and a half hacking a stairway out of the wall of snow that still buried the easy horse trail to the pass. And in 1968 the snow was so deep through the summer that the old trail was virtually abandoned for a newer route up a warmer south-facing headwall.

Turning now toward this newer route the packstring ambles across a meadow that embraces a chain of ponds called, rather grandly, Cottonwood Lakes. One of the riders dismounts to ease the agony of city-soft muscles congealed in the unfamiliar contours of a Western saddle and to take a drink from a lake. The water is sweet and pure, but no more so than the air, which has been warming in the late-morning sun and now caresses the meadow in a movement that is no longer a wind, only a stirring. Here beneath the summit peaks is a sharpness of light that seems to surround everything, bringing out each subtle texture and color tone. And the air is so clean that every leaf and pebble and flake of bark and blade of grass is sharply delineated, every shadow drawn as with a needle. Mark Twain took note of this, too: "The air up there...is very pure and fine, bracing and delicious," he wrote. "And why shouldn't it be?—it is the same the angels breathe."

The horsemen begin the last climb to the crest of the pass, over a rough, narrow set of switchbacks that zigzag for some 800 vertical feet across a fall of boulders and rocks. At the highest, most tenuous spot near the top a rider dismounts to unhitch the lead ropes that have secured one animal to the next. Two mules fell here not long ago, down into the rocks; and there is no desire now to repeat the performance, with perhaps the whole packstring being peeled off the trail like a rope of rock-climbers snatched from a precipice by one falling comrade. Abruptly, the horses top the final rise. And there, in a great arc from north to west, is the wild, austere sweep of the High Sierra heartland.

Wave upon wave of granitic rock—granodiorite, quartz monzonite, and granite—has been heaved and tossed and eroded here into the most dramatic stretch of wilderness anywhere in the old continental United States. At every point in the arc the eye is overwhelmed by the immensity of rock, the presence of rock, the height, the shape and the enormous power of rock that dominates this land. Across the first saddle, a bare beige dip of weathered outcrop, is 14,042-foot Mount Langley, its flattish crown notched from the tumbling out of granitic blocks split off by the brutal action of winter frost. From Langley the other crags of the Sierra crest rise in terrible sawteeth to the summit of 14,494-foot Mount Whitney, climax of the Sierra wilderness and the tallest mountain in the old 48 states. To the west the brown barrens sweep down to the timber above Rock Creek. Then the land sinks into the ruler-straight trough of Kern Canyon, rises onto the gravelly, pine-wooded terrace of Chagoopa Plateau to climax once more in the red and black spires of the Kaweah Peaks—the tallest nearly 14,000 feet and molded in relief by smoke from a lowland forest fire.

Within sight of these mountains are a half dozen others soaring above 14,000 feet. And off beyond the horizon to the north stands a ragged rank of some 500 peaks above 12,000 feet, their crowns laced with mini-glaciers and crescents of lingering snow. Along the line of mountains the heights are slashed from east to west by glacial gorges whose granitic walls plunge farther than those of any other canyons in North America: at the foot of Junction Ridge, where the South and Middle Forks of the Kings River come brawling together, the defile drops 8,200 feet to the stream bed, deeper by 2,000 feet than the Grand Canyon.

Ninety-five miles to the north, past the pumice-strewn cone of Mammoth Mountain and the dark volcanic spires of the Minarets, is the bold drama of the Yosemite, whose precipices rise even more abruptly than those of Kings Canyon, though not so high. Here the Merced River is born in a moonscape of granitic rock where little will grow but lichen and moss and mattings of stunted whitebark pine. Here, too, as in the bowl by the Cottonwood Lakes and all through the high country, the rock is so hard, so enduring that in many places even the grinding force of the glaciers could not disturb it. Instead the moving ice could only scour and polish so that in a certain slant of sun whole mountainsides shine too brightly for the eye to endure for more than a few seconds at a time. Below these mirrors of stone the tributaries of the Merced meet in an abyss of bedrock. Farther down, the riverbanks, looping through a meadow some seven miles long, are guarded by tall ponderosa pine and sweetened by the fragrance of incense cedar. Nowhere in the world is a more beautiful valley than this, flanked by walls of monolithic rock that rise on either side from 3,000 to 4,800 feet above the meadow—El Capitan, Glacier Point, Sentinel Rock, Half Dome—laced with half a dozen waterfalls: the highest, Yosemite, tumbles and free-falls 2,565 feet (Niagara is only 167 feet) to join the Merced.

Yet throughout the Sierra there are other sights just as captivating, though perhaps more fleeting and subtler. On the western edge of the range the foothills take a slow upward rise from the San Joaquin Valley. Then beginning at Visalia, 75 miles south of Fresno, the land rolls and pitches 45 miles eastward through a series of powerful folds to the heights of the Great Western Divide. The average gradient on this western slope is only 6 per cent—about 300 feet to the mile. Yet as a traveler gradually gains altitude he becomes aware of a steady drop in the temperature and a corresponding change in the whole look of the land as he moves upward from the subtropical heat of the valley to the relative chill among the peaks. In certain places, particularly along the steeper river courses, this climatic shift is so pronounced that on a recent December morning inside the canyon of the Middle Fork of the Kaweah River a single sweep of the eye could take in a weather show that might have unfolded from Florida to Alaska.

Down on the river bottom, where the altitude is no more than 800 feet above sea level, a thunderstorm was moving across grassy hillocks and stands of sycamore trees. At 1,700 feet a camper, comfortable in a light sweater, stood at the edge of a field of live oak and tarweed, spattered by random drops of temperate rain. On the north side of the canyon a tall rock dotted by maples was in fog, dank at the cloud bottom, a hint of chill rolling down the slope. Across the canyon another higher peak was dusted by snow that grew visibly deeper until the mountain

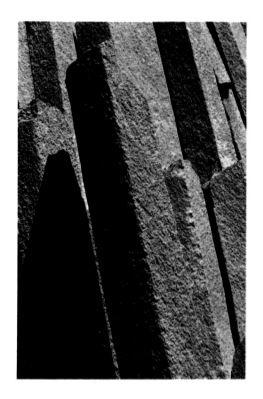

In their precision and symmetry, the gray basalt shafts above—part of the Devils Postpile in the central Sierra—look as if they had been carved in a sculptor's studio. Actually the obelisks were formed some four million years ago when a lava flow, cooling and shrinking, developed vertical cracks; subsequent erosion and glacial action exposed the pillars. Such basaltic outcroppings are common, and this symmetry of cracking is not unusual.

disappeared into its own cloud covering. And in a burst of sunlight at the head of the gorge shone the massif of Mount Stewart, its glacier buried beneath a blanket of wind-crusted snow.

Blended into the setting for this climatic spectrum stands an extravagant race of trees, native only to the moist western slope of the Sierra. And a visitor moving into the wilderness comes upon them almost by chance as the way climbs up the northern edge of Kaweah Canyon. Suddenly, set back in the forest will be a tree trunk perhaps 14 feet across. The massive shaft, its cinnamon-red bark fluted like a Grecian column, rises bare of branches for perhaps 90 feet to disappear into the canopy of white fir and sugar pine clustered in attendance about its waist. Above those lesser trees, themselves more than 100 feet tall, the great creature crowns at a height of 200 feet or more. Botanists classify these trees as *Sequoiadendron giganteum*; old Sierra hands know them, more humbly, as the Big Trees. Either name is correct. For the giant sequoias are the largest living things on earth. And this particular giant is one of the younger, smaller members of the family.

There are 3,500 more here in a single grove called Giant Forest, with another 13,000 in scattered stands nearby and north to Yosemite and beyond. Everything about them is on a heroic scale, so much so that a first-time visitor tends to lose any sense of proportion and must stand among them awhile to absorb their true size. In any mature grove the most ordinary are 20 feet in diameter; and the very largest measure 35 to 40 feet through—enough to block a city street from curb to curb. Their bark is as much as two feet thick and deeply scarred by ground fires that raced through the forest in years past, cleaning out the lesser growth and leaving black gnawings among the root buttresses of the Big Trees. The branches, where they begin to occur high overhead, are heavy, twisted, bullish, ungraceful, yet they taper into smoke puffs of evergreen leaves as delicate as those of a young cedar, with tiny cones no bigger than a baby's fist. No one knows when these regal monsters first germinated, but probably they have been growing for 3,500 years or more. A few are over 300 feet tall, though the tops of many older trees have been blasted off by lightning as they reared above the surrounding forest centuries ago. The smell that fills these groves is the rich, dry scent of ripe redwood shavings, the redwood being the coastal cousin— *Sequoia sempervirens*—of the Big Tree. And the sound of the wind in the sequoias' crowns is high and soft and distant, like the rush of a cataract far off, a sound of prehistory, agonizingly pure and haunting, a sigh from a lost time when there were no human beings here.

It is, in all, a land of primeval grandeur, this High Sierra; of granitic crags striated by avalanche gullies; of trees tortured and dwarfed at timber line but superbly tall in the forests below; of scores of booming cascades and nearly 2,000 mountain lakes and ponds, each resting in its cup of granitic rock or of flower-speckled meadow grass. It is a land that has remained in many ways as wild as it was 200 years ago when the Spanish missionary Fray Pedro Font first spied its gleaming peaks from the west and named it *una gran sierra nevada* (a great snowy range). It is a land still browsed by bands of bighorn sheep and mule deer, a land prowled by the mountain lion and the pine marten and watched over by the lordly golden eagle.

That this high country has survived so well as wilderness is due very much to its formidable geology. For the Sierra splits the state of California for 400 longitudinal miles from just below Lassen Peak in the north down to the petering out into cactus flats near the town of Mojave in the south. From the earliest days of exploration these mountains, which rise at Whitney to a wall standing two full miles above the valley, have been a redoubtable barrier to those who felt they had to enter them (the Indians, more sensible about such things, rarely bothered, except for the urgent business of trade or hunting or war—and then only in the best days of summer).

John Charles Frémont, the celebrated trailblazer, political adventurer and gold speculator, reduced an aged Indian to tears of commiseration by asking in the bleak January of 1844 just how a man might cross these ridges at the gentler elevations southwest of Lake Tahoe. The trail was very hard, replied the Indian—six sleeps in summer, and in winter one should not go at all: "Rock on rock, snow on snow," he chanted, "and even if you get over the snow you will not be able to get down from the mountain." Frémont went nonetheless, and did manage to make it over the snow and down the mountain, but not until he had been so thoroughly blizzard-bound and starved that his party had to slaughter and eat virtually everything on four legs, including their pet dog Tlamath. It was three years later and barely 40 miles away that a party of emigrants, led by an injudicious man named George Donner, found itself even more hard pressed and resorted to more bizarre fare: "Mrs. Murphy said here yesterday," noted one of the party in a diary, "that she thought she would commence on Milton and eat him, I do not think she has done so yet, it is so distressing. . . ."

Though the menu for visitors has improved, these mountains are not always easy to cross even today. From Pyramid Peak, where the 10,000-foot-elevations of the true high country begin just below Donner Pass, to the edge of the Kern Plateau south of Whitney, only five winding paved roads have been cut through, and four of those are snowed shut from November to May or June. There is one stretch of 160 crow-flight miles running north from the Kern country to Tuolumne Meadows on the eastern edge of Yosemite with no roads at all, only footpaths and horse trails twisting up to passes hacked out of the granitic rock at altitudes up to 13,600 feet.

It has taken more than an accident of geology, however, to keep this wilderness from vanishing under the sooty blanket of civilization. California, with nearly 24 million people in 1980, is the most populous state and one of the fastest growing. Each year over a fourth of the population, reinforced by armies of out-of-staters, crowds into the Sierra to sightsee or go camping. And of these, perhaps two million tread on some corner of the real high country. Yet, with some woeful exceptions, that tread has remained comparatively light. For in acts of wisdom and foresight rare in an ambitious, basically exploitative people, the High Sierra has been placed in the protective embrace of nine national forests and three enormous national parks, Yosemite—which is bigger than the state of Rhode Island—and the contiguous Sequoia and Kings Canyon Parks, together even larger and the major seedbed for the Big Trees. Certain enclaves along the rivers have been given over to the lowland cities for reservoirs; limited sections are open to either supervised timber cutting, livestock grazing or the operation of tourist facilities—all of which infuriate the lovers of primitive land. But most of the Sierra back country is essentially wild. And there are some 2,138,000 acres within the national forests that have been designated by Congress under the Wilderness Act of 1964 to be preserved as Wilderness with a capital "W," a place where man may come only as a visitor and leave the land exactly as he finds it—in the natural state of things.

The Wilderness Act was a sweet triumph in a foot-slogging hundred years' war by American conservationists. So far the act has guaranteed the preservation for all time of 79.8 million wild acres. In folding such land under its wing, the act formally defines a Wilderness as an area "retaining its primeval character and influence, without permanent improvements or human habitation and which generally appears to have been affected primarily by the forces of nature, with the imprint of man's work substantially unnoticeable (and which) has outstanding opportunities for solitude or a primitive and unconfined type of recreation." The act also contains a statement of policy, a sort of preamble, whose basic message marks the end point of nearly 400 years in the evolution of attitudes toward the wilderness in American society: "It is hereby declared to be the policy of the Congress to secure for the American people of present and future generations the benefits of an enduring resource of wilderness. . . ."

That is not the way either the government or much of its constituency has historically looked upon the wilderness.

The more common reflex, that of the Western pioneers upon being confronted with such wild vistas, was to shoot anything that moved, chop down anything that grew, and salivate over the profits to be grubbed from the primeval soil. By 1850, following a series of gold strikes among the Sierra foothills and neighboring ranges, 100,000 men had come scrambling in, dredging and damming streams, killing Indians and each other, and generally making a mess of whatever they touched. As the land opened up, livestock drovers grazed some three million head of cattle and nearly six million sheep through the mountains, stripping the high meadows. Hunters decimated wild bands of bighorn sheep, elk and antelope; predators such as wolves or grizzlies were edged toward extinction under the banner of civilization.

But even then a few quiet voices were beginning to suggest that there was more to be had from a wilderness than targets and treasure. Emerson said, "In the wilderness, I find something more dear and connate than in the streets or villages . . . in the woods we return to reason and faith." And a Massachusetts poet and lover of the ways of wild things, Henry David Thoreau, was asking a persistent and practical question: "Why should not we . . . have our national preserves . . . in which the bear and panther, and some even of the hunter race, may still exist, and not be 'civilized off the face of the earth'—our forests . . . not for idle sport or food, but for inspiration and our own true recreation?"

Incredibly for those rapacious times a few powerful men listened to such voices; and in 1864 Congress passed a bill ceding Yosemite Valley to the state of California as a park, the first such wild preserve to be set aside by federal action anywhere in America, "for public use, resort and recreation." Unfortunately, the young state did not provide adequate protection to the area. One of the park's early visitors was 30-year-old John Muir, a Scotsman who arrived leading a band of 2,050 hungry sheep. He soon realized that grazing sheep and cattle were devastating the lovely mountain meadows, and that illegal logging was stripping away the precious giant trees. Muir stayed on to become a devout conservationist and tireless chronicler of the natural wonders of the Sierra.

With Emerson and Thoreau, Muir believed that in wilderness lay truth and man's salvation ("Climb the mountains and get their good tidings. Nature's peace will flow into you as sunshine flows into trees. The winds will blow their own freshness into you, and the storms their energy, while cares will drop off like autumn leaves"). This messianic spirit shines from Muir's surviving portraits; his bearded face seems always in repose, with a soft light of almost celestial understanding showing in the eye—the quintessential naturalist. Yet he was an awesomely energetic man whose passion for his beloved Sierra led him to such eccentricities as shinnying to the top of a 100-foot pine in the teeth of a gale to be closer to the song of the wind in the needles, and bounding from the door of his cabin during a cataclysmic wrench of the Sierra bedrock, shouting joyously, "A noble earthquake, a noble earthquake!"

Muir would disappear into the high country for days at a time, fortified by a crust of bread and his conviction that nothing truly bad could ever happen in the mountains. The notes gathered on these forays, and later published, were scientifically perceptive and his prose was lyrical enough to awaken a small but vociferous segment of the electorate, though the phrases ranged in quality from the sweetest poesy to the most effusive 19th Century goo ("happy mountain raindrops . . . kissing the lips of lilies!"). He was the first to record the existence of glaciers in the Sierra and to deduce the true effect of ancient ice upon the contours of Yosemite; he compiled detailed observations on the Sierra's creatures and its trees, particularly the sugar pines, which he worshipfully described as the "priests of the pines"; he rhapsodized upon storms and meadows and waterfalls; and he was endlessly fascinated by a peculiar bird called the water ouzel, which has the odd habit of diving under water and walking about on the bottom in search of food, emitting bubbles from its nostrils.

Muir's preachments upon the Sierra and the need to preserve its wilderness caught the conservationist ear of Teddy Roosevelt, and Muir became a prime mover in the expansion of Yosemite as a public preserve and the transfer of the valley back to federal jurisdiction. Muir originated the idea for another major park named Sequoia, now jointly administered with the adjacent Kings Canyon National Park. He helped prepare the soil in which the seeds of both the National Park and National Forest Services were planted; and by the time of his death in 1914, he had become a kind of spiritual monument to the whole con-

Photographed at dawn, a stretch of the Sierra includes 14,494-foot Mount Whitney (right, rear) and the Alabama Hills (foreground).

servation movement, the deep and secret self-image of everyone who would go up into the hills with a pack on his back and an eye on the shining rock of the Sierra crest.

However, Muir and company might be a trifle stunned at a few other consequences of their crusade and would unquestionably have trouble recognizing some of their disciples. The more than 10 million visitors who come to the Sierra in peak years arrive in scores of different guises and with nearly as many different motives. At Yosemite, which trembles under the impact of about one third of the Sierra's total visitors, 90 per cent are auto-borne sightseers who stay for a few days in the franchised motels or the wooden-floored tent communities; they snap a few pictures, perhaps try a guided trail ride from the dude stables, or buy a load of precut wood to toss onto the bonfire at a community sing. In an effort to reduce traffic on its roads, Yosemite Park offers free rides to sightseers on handsome buses that shuttle from parking lots to various points of interest. There are also more extensive guided tours available. But most of the sightseers, lured to the area by its reputation and by its relative convenience to heavily populated metropolitan areas of California, arrive to experience only a brief and superficial encounter with the beauty of Yosemite. There are still a few such as the visitor who was heard to snarl at her husband, "Now I don't want to hear NOTHIN' about flora, fauna or geology, understand?"

The founding fathers of the wilderness never envisioned the sort of bustle that exists not only at Yosemite but at Sequoia and Kings Canyon, where an annual mass of two million or more crunch elbows for a quick look at the Big Trees. The crowd brings its drug and money problems and leaves its exhaust smoke and litter behind; a federal magistrate at park headquarters levies fines and issues sentences for speeding, writing rubber checks, smoking pot and defacing trees.

Yet Yosemite Valley and the beaten-down portals at Sequoia and Kings Canyon represent no more than 24 square miles in a parkland total of 2,503, most of it high wilderness opening directly onto the roadless sweep of the Sierra's back country. Right at the edge of Yosemite Valley a pathway called the John Muir Trail takes off into the heart of the mountains and rambles southward for 212 miles to terminate atop Mount Whitney, never touching pavement and never dropping below 7,500 feet once it leaves the Yosemite area. At Wallace Creek near Mount Whitney the Muir Trail connects with the High Sierra Trail, another wild route, leading 80 miles to Giant Forest. Radiating from these two arteries is a loose pattern of 3,000 more miles of horse- and footpaths. In recent years no fewer than 500,000 high-country campers —backpackers and horsemen—have set out upon them to fish the clear lakes, to walk among the wild flowers of summer meadows, to sleep in tents or in sleeping bags beneath the stars, restoring themselves by living for a night or a full summer as part of the wild land.

Not all of them do so with grace. The number of wilderness users has been going up steadily every year, so that a few parts of even the high country are in danger of being trampled into a sylvan slum by the very people who go there to love it. "We're first in the nation in the number of campers," says a national forest supervisor, with a mixture of pride and dismay. "Today," explains one Yosemite ranger, "a guy with a Sears, Roebuck card can, with a stroke of his pen, buy a complete camper outfit and come up here. He doesn't have the faintest idea of how to use that equipment, or what he's doing. And yet he's just as much of a camper as John Muir, and has every bit as much right to use the wilderness."

The Sierra makes no such allowances. Occasionally the mountains will lash out and take a life when someone is inexperienced or really careless in the high country. Not long ago a woman, a newcomer to the wilderness, tried to cool her feet in a stream that was booming with the snow melt of June. She was swept away and her husband went in to save her. By the wildest luck she caught a rock downstream and pulled herself out; but her husband's body was never found.

Though the lethal potential is always there, the High Sierra is most often kind to its pilgrims, particularly those who treat it with care. And most people do. The typical back-country camper, according to a survey distributed by the Department of Agriculture, is someone used to the wilderness and its ways, someone who has been there before and will go again, with family members or close friends. In the Sierra today there is at least an 80 percent chance that the camper is a backpacker; three decades ago "75 to 80 per cent were on horses," says a Forest Service official. "But today you've got a generation that hasn't been brought up around horses; they're not used to them, scared of them, maybe. And I think, too, it has to do with this desire of people to be completely free, independent, not tied to the packstring or anything."

The back-country visitor will stay out for five or six days. And whether on horse or foot the camper will be there basically to do as John Muir did—to let the beautiful days enrich life and saturate themselves into every part of the body. A typical camper is someone like the fireman from Alhambra, California, who went onto the Muir Trail recently with his two sons, 11 and 13, to make a special, sentimental journey: he had done the Muir once before in 1937 at the age of 12, and now there was the precious dividend of seeing it again through eyes so young.

Other campers are adventurers, such as the handsome young couple who were spotted coming down the Echo Lake trail one morning not long ago. "We're part of a survival class from Berkeley," said the boy, shifting the weight of his backpack. Rarely have two people survived more successfully than this pair, who glowed with good health and whose emergency rations remained untouched after four days out. They had been living on trout caught on bent pins, then roasted on a stick and spiced with algae common to the local lakes. "We read about it in a book," said the girl, "and it was real great."

Such high-country devotees show a remarkably similar attachment to the Sierra, a kind of mystical devotion that takes some time to germinate. For the heartland of this wilderness is, upon first view, not only dramatic but harsh and bare and somewhat forbidding. "You have to let it soak in before you understand this Sierra mystique, what it is," says a Sequoia Park ranger who has spent his life in the mountains. "There's a starkness to this high country; you realize that the plants and animals are right on the margin of existence, and hanging on. And," he adds, "you can't help but marvel at it."

Every Sierra lover seems to share this compulson to explain the special lure of the wilderness so that others will know and understand it and love it as he loves it. But in his heart he does not want any new people to go there or to bring their friends. Because like most passions the love of wilderness tends to be a selfish and a self-centered thing. And every new person is another set of footprints on a trail, another ring of blackened campfire rocks, another flash of a red backpack or an orange tent on a trail or by a lake that the Sierra lover wants exclusively, on that hour of that day, and preferably forever. For this is the part of the Sierra that a devotee is willing to share only with close companions, to see, to use, to savor. Almost anyone else appears to be an intruder.

As one of those horsemen on the Cottonwood trail in Indian summer, I can tell you for certain that it is my Sierra. And I tell you, very selfishly, this: I wish no one had ever been here before.

I wish I had been the first man ever to crest New Army Pass and see that wild sweep of Sierra, the first to have heard the wind in the crown of a giant sequoia, the first to have tasted the sweet water in the pools below the falls at Yosemite. But since that cannot be, I will tell you how I like my Sierra now. I like it from horseback. And I like it in the fall when you and all your friends have gone, when the nights are frost-cold and the days warm, the bright gold of aspen leaves backlit by a slant of equinoctial sun. I like it, perhaps most of all, as it was on the afternoon following the ride up from Cottonwood Canyon.

At 4:30 in the afternoon a cold wind was blowing down from the summit of Mount Whitney, across the wooded meadow where we had made camp. Two of us resaddled our horses and rode up to a lake that lies in the enormous granitic bowl below the west face of Whitney. A doe herded her pair of almost identical fawns along the trail ahead of us for a time and then turned them into a copse of willow to stand perfectly still, watching us as we rode by. Around a nose of rock the headwall of the mountain came into view, far above timber, gullied and slashed by avalanche tracks. To its left was the pinnacle of Mount Russell, one of the last major peaks in the Sierra to be climbed—and the taker of at least one climber's life. To the right was a palisade whose flanks, like Whitney's, were scored by avalanches. And this same palisade extended around the sky in an unbroken ridge, curving up from the south to embrace Whitney's summit, then around toward Russell and finally tapering down close to the trail on our left.

The sun was lowering toward the Kaweah Peaks when our horses pulled down their heads to drink at the edge of the lake, and the sundown wind was becoming colder and stronger. We dismounted, turned up our collars and left the animals, to walk among the rocks and boulders. The lake's feeder stream was dried to a trickle, but in years past it has been so filled with spawning trout that their backs stood out of water. As we watched the play of wind upon the lake, the sun impaled itself upon the Kaweahs and the refracted light deepened the relief of every crevice, every pinnacle. The last rays combed through yellowing willows and shone dazzling on the polished rock. As the shadow moved up to envelop the lesser heights, only the crown of Whitney was left in sun. And over the space of 15 minutes that crown turned from a luminescent yellow white to burnt orange to the magic lavender of alpenglow, and abruptly to the forbidding slate gray of evening. Then we turned to remount for the ride down, and there appeared by a horse's hoof the perfect counterpoint to all this grandeur, a tiny blue flower—whorled penstemon—barely two inches above the ground, as small and delicate as the mountains were stark and overpowering. It was a perfect sunset in the Sierra, and the sky was a smear of stars as we unsaddled our horses back at camp and turned them out to graze for the night.

The Age of John Muir

In 1901, the outdoor enthusiasts of the Sierra Club planned their first camping trip through the high country. Female members received detailed advice: "Skirts can be short, not more than half way from knee to ankle, and under them can be worn shorter dark-colored bloomers.... For the women who ride horseback, divided skirts are recommended."

The 21-day expedition delighted John Muir (opposite), president of the Sierra Club since its founding in 1892. The outing also pointed up the tremendous changes that had taken place in Muir's beloved Sierra in his own lifetime. Until the late 1840s, when Muir was brought to America as an 11-year-old Scottish immigrant, the range was a fearsome barrier, little known and seldom penetrated by white men. By the 1860s, when Muir came to live in Yosemite Valley, the Sierra was being mapped and exploited. Now, in 1901, the mountains were judged safe enough for female Sierra Clubbers, who were confidently expected to hike up to 20 miles a day.

These dramatic changes had been set in motion by the discovery of gold on the American River in 1848. Ragtag hordes of prospectors, followed by mining companies, worked their way upstream from the Sierra foothills. The crude mining camps swelled into raucous boomtowns served by railroads. By 1870, with comfortable trains giving access to the wild interior, tourists were arriving in ever-increasing numbers to marvel at the scenery.

But the landscape, even then, was being violated. Loggers left great fields of stumps. Mining companies diverted rivers and leveled whole hills. Mountain meadows were overgrazed by sheep—"hoofed locusts," Muir called them—that crowded out the wild creatures.

The exploiters got no quarter from John Muir. His antisheep broadsides were largely responsible for the 1890 and 1906 acts of Congress that created Yosemite and Sequoia National Parks. As late as 1913, a year before his death, Muir led a campaign against plans to build a reservoir in Hetch Hetchy Valley. He lost that last fight, but his lifework left broad expanses of unspoiled Sierra wilderness, virginal places that proved the wisdom of his creed: "Everyone needs beauty as well as bread."

Naturalist John Muir, 70 years old and still going strong, pauses in Yosemite in 1908 to scan his well-loved mountains. His nature studies took him as far as Alaska, Russia, India and Australia, but he always returned to the Sierra, his spiritual home.

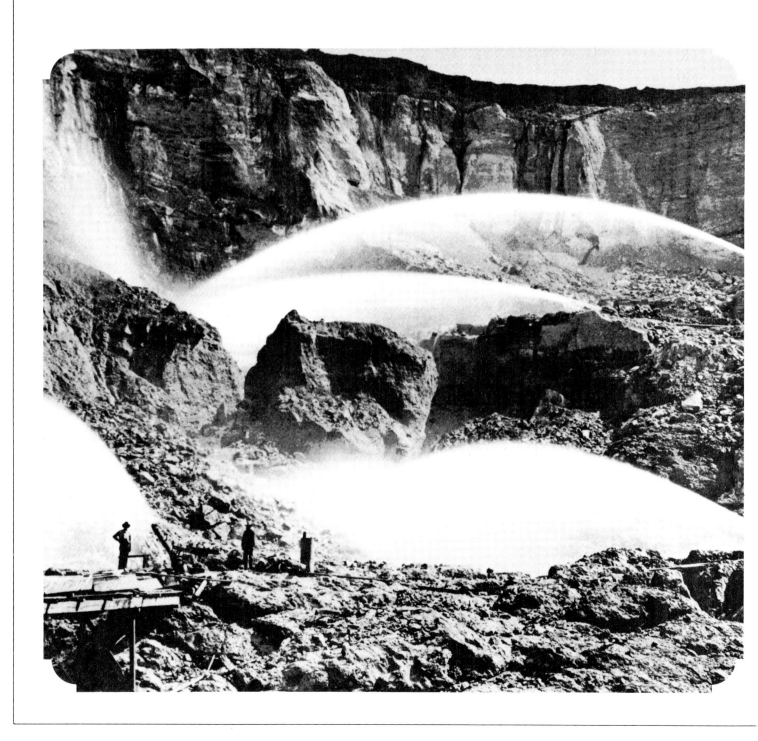

Rich Gold Strikes and Hungry Prospectors

The early days of the Gold Rush produced a bumper crop of wondrous success stories, some of them true. For 11 days in a row, four miners averaged $1,250 a day working a claim only six feet by 10 feet. Others unearthed supernuggets of pure gold, each weighing 20 pounds or more, and many panned enough gold dust, at $18 an ounce, to shower touring dancers with bags worth a small fortune. But most freelance prospectors had trouble making ends meet at inflated gold-camp prices. The majority's lot was glumly summed up by Adolphus Windeler, a German sailor turned prospector: "Hard times, hard work, & little gold."

Generally, the men who mined for pay fared better. Once a "hydraulic" mining company located paydirt, its high-pressure water hoses would collapse whole cliffs and direct the debris into long sluice runs that processed tons of material each day. The Malakoff mine at North Bloomfield sifted $4 million in gold out of 41 million cubic yards of earth in 22 years; and if its hired hands never got rich, at least they ate regularly.

Mining the newfangled hydraulic way, pipemen at the mile-long Malakoff pit aim high-pressure hoses to blast loose gold-bearing sand and gravel. The jets of water, directed from nozzles known as Little Giants, were powerful enough to kill a man at a range of 200 feet.

Panning for gold in the 1850s, a group of freelance prospectors sifts through silt on a Sierra riverbank. Such groups often bought food and supplies in common and split the cost. But many a miner down on his luck had to pay his share by doing odd jobs or working part time for a local mining company.

Whitney's Band of Bold Surveyors

In 1860, the California legislature set up an agency to survey the state and collect samples of all its resources. Scientific knowledge was only part of the legislators' purpose; they also hoped that the survey would find gold. Headed by a cantankerous geologist named Josiah Whitney, the venture ran out of funds before completing its task. But Whitney's group did map the High Sierra, until then largely unknown.

Most of the Sierra exploration was done by six enthusiastic experts who started their work in 1863. Their first field leader was William Brewer, a shrewd, courageous botanist. The most colorful surveyor was Clarence King, who published melodramatic accounts of his exploits: " 'We're in for it now, King,' remarked my companion . . . but our blood was up, and danger added only an exhilarating thrill. . . ." However, King suppressed such frills in his official reports. Describing the truly dangerous ascent of 14,018-foot-high Mount Tyndall, he wrote, "The summit was reached, without serious difficulty, after some risky climbing."

Charles Hoffmann, a German-born engineer who acted as field chief of the survey in 1867, sets up his transit near the summit of the Sierra mountain named after him. His maps of the range established a cartographic standard that long outlasted the survey itself.

When the California Geological Survey began its official exploration of the Sierra in 1863, its members were, from left, Chester Averell, William More Gabb, William Ashburner, director Josiah D. Whitney, Charles F. Hoffmann, Clarence King and William H. Brewer. In 14 years of existence, the survey was often left short of funds by the state; the last of its many publications, a Yosemite guidebook, was printed at Whitney's own expense.

Dowd's Grove of Tall Timber

In 1852 a hunter named A. T. Dowd came upon a grove of trees so huge that his report of what he had seen was laughed off as a tall tale. Days later Dowd lured a few miners up to the grove, and crowed, "Now, boys, do you believe my big tree story?"

Dowd's report attracted widespread attention to the Sierra's sequoias, now known to be the largest living plants on earth. Though commercial logging operations did not begin in earnest until the 1860s, the wondrous size of Dowd's trees immediately attracted eager promoters whom John Muir called "laborious vandals." One stripped the bark off a live sequoia and displayed it in New York as "The Tree Mastodon: a mountain of wood." Another shill built a two-lane bowling alley atop a recumbent giant. The stump of a third sequoia was put to several uses. Smoothed off and roofed over, it served as a ballroom (for up to 48 dancers) and later as a stage for theatrical performances. Then in 1858, it housed the press and staff of a short-lived newspaper, *The Big Tree Bulletin and Murphys Advertiser.*

Loggers celebrate the felling of a giant sequoia with a solemn picture-taking ceremony. This tree, 26 feet in diameter at the base, yielded some 370,000 board feet of lumber—roughly enough to crate the liner Queen Elizabeth II.

A Railroad Built despite Rock and Snow

The Central Pacific Railroad opened the way for large-scale Sierra tourism when it began building eastward from Sacramento on January 8, 1863. Its route, curling 140 miles through the Sierra by way of Emigrant Gap, was enormously difficult. Ravines had to be filled in, mountainsides cut and as many as 15 tunnels blasted through solid granitic rock. Deep snowfall almost baffled the engineers. If the snowfall was not too heavy, pilot locomotives fitted with wedge-shaped snowplows kept the track cleared, but storm-born avalanches could sometimes stop even a plow-equipped steam engine that had several others pushing behind it.

The solution was to build roofs over the track at danger points. In the course of three years, crews used millions of board feet of lumber to construct 40 miles of snowsheds, inspiring one old trainman to remark that this was the first time he had ever "railroaded in a barn." But the barns did the job. In April 1868, the first train steamed through the Sierra and headed toward the East.

Eight locomotives puff away to push a ponderous snowplow through high drifts below Donner Pass in 1890. Because light snowplows were often derailed by the drifts, weight was gradually added. The heaviest plow weighed more than 19 tons, and as many as 11 locomotives got behind it.

Above Yosemite, two open-sided stagecoaches climb the switchbacks of Big Oak Flat Road, bound for Stockton. By 1903, when the picture was taken, the first automobiles were visiting the valley—and panicking the local livestock. The result: Cars were banned from Yosemite Valley until 1913.

Early Days in Hutchings' Eden

Rumors of lofty cliffs and waterfalls lured the first real tourist to Yosemite Valley in 1855. He was James M. Hutchings, an English-born journalist, and his florid travel articles about the valley attracted other sightseers. In Yosemite, Hutchings found both a passion and a profitable career. To accommodate the visitors, he bought and improved the Upper Hotel in the 1860s.

The future of tourism was assured in 1874, when two routes to the gold fields, the Big Oak Flat Road and the Coulterville Road, were extended on into the valley, permitting visitors to come by stagecoach.

When the coaches arrived, Hutchings' teen-aged daughter Florence, a reckless tomboy nicknamed Squirrel, acted as unofficial greeter. She would gallop out to meet the stagecoaches and race them back to the hotel. This performance scandalized some guests almost as much as the sight of Florence smoking a pipe.

Visitors to the valley in 1900 enjoy a pastoral jaunt against the backdrop of Yosemite Falls. A half century of tourism had raised the annual influx of sightseers to 10,000 and removed the earlier risks and discomforts of travel into the Sierra. The first visitors, proud of their daring and their purple prose, had braved bad roads and bad men to describe waterfalls as "living light from heaven" and themselves as "fearless spirits and noble hearted fellows."

Pausing in a forest grove, members of John Muir's Sierra Club enjoy an elaborate picnic during their annual outing in 1903.

2/ A Country Standing on End

*The signature of the glaciers is almost everywhere in the
Sierra — on almost every lake shore, every
headwall, every pass — for those who have eyes to see.*
WILLIAM O. DOUGLAS/ *MY WILDERNESS*

Not many years ago, a Sequoia National Park ranger strolled into the
middle of a crowd of some 300 adventurous souls who had made a Labor
Day climb from the Owens Valley to the flattish rock table that marks
the summit of Mount Whitney. One hiker, awed by the sight of the two-
mile plunge down to the valley floor, asked the ranger if he knew how
the Sierra came to be shaped as it is.

"Well," said the ranger, who had a smattering of geology, "this summit plateau is part of the old landscape that was lying here as kind of a
rolling lowland millions of years ago. Then the whole Sierra was pushed
up as a block along faults immediately to the east." As he talked, other
people turned to listen. "As the bedrock moved upward, small sections
of the earth's crust dropped downward, forming depressions like the
Owens Valley. And later, through erosion and glaciation we got the final
shaping of the land—the meadows and canyons and peaks and bowls—
as you see them all around you today."

The ranger had paused to let that sink in, when a voice came from the
crowd: "I don't believe anything you say. The Bible said the Lord made
the world in six days, so nothing you say is true."

"Well, yes it does; it says that," replied the ranger, thoughtfully, and
wandered off by himself to ponder the ultimate nature of geologic truth.
Months later he had still not thought of a more suitable reply. "What
could I tell the guy?" he shrugged. "Besides, maybe he was right."

Maybe he was. Today the most sophisticated earth scientists are still groping among the particulars of the Sierra's creation. Some of those particulars (e.g., the role of sea-floor spreading in the Sierra's growth, the migration of silicon ions in the chemical weathering of certain types of rock) are complex indeed. The wilderness traveler need not think too much about them. But the main part of the Sierra story is as bold and dramatic as the mountains themselves. The evidence of mountain building and sculpturing is sticking right up where anyone can see it and shows in such a way that even the least-informed visitor can scarcely help becoming involved. It is all but impossible to look at Half Dome in Yosemite *(page 65)* and not wonder how it got that way: a 4,800-foot mass of granitic rock whose face is a perpendicular wall and whose evenly rounded back would make a perfect mold for a massive concert shell. His first glimpse of the 10,895-foot wall of the Mount Whitney scarp so stirred Albrecht Penck, doyen of European geologists in the World War I era, that he asked to be left alone for some time that he might contemplate it in silence. Nor is it necessary to go to the Sierra's showplaces, since the landscape along almost any trail in the high wilderness is a beautifully disordered tableau of the Sierra's past, and all of it a part of the living present.

Near the waist of the Sierra, for example, there is a narrow path that climbs to a glacial bowl beneath the pinnacles of the Silver Divide. No guided tours go there. In fact, hardly anyone goes there at all, for the bowl lies several rough miles from any main trail, and the summit country around it has the angry look of land abandoned by growing things. The bowl holds no glacier now, just snow remnants that endure through late summer, and in the bottom a deep green lake called Anne. I rode there one afternoon from a meadow campground farther down to get as far away as possible from every sign of people. The higher I rode, the closer I felt to the heart of the Sierra and the more intrigued I became by the circumstances of the mountains' origin and evolution.

According to the widely accepted geological theory of plate tectonics, all mountains are the result of the interplay of fundamental forces in the earth's outer shell, and the underlying mantle, which is composed of semimolten rock. Some mountains grow from the protracted eruption of molten material that gives rise to volcanoes. In this instance, the molten material rises through the outer shell and emerges on its surface as lava and/or ash. Other mountains are the result of compressions that make the earth's crust contract in such a way that massive wrinkles called folds appear, or huge blocks break apart and move past each other along fracture lines called faults. The basic materials from which the bedrock of some mountains originally came may be sediments from ancient sea bottoms, including vast accumulations of fossilized marine organisms. They may be the outpourings of volcanoes, or they may be molten bulges of rock called intrusions, which well up and push aside the overlying rock or penetrate its crevices and weak spots. During its creation a mountain range may be eroded into V-shaped valleys by streams, gouged further into U-shaped valleys by glaciers, honed into exotic shapes by wind, or quarried into pinnacles and blocks by the freezing and thawing of water. The Sierra is a living stage for virtually all these phenomena, which interacted in the past to create the range as it is today—and which are still contending to make the mountains into whatever they will be during some geologic tomorrow.

The lower trail to center stage at Anne Lake led out of a pine wood onto fields of smooth gray-white granitic rock. Scattered about in the open were truck-sized boulders of a beige tinge, a different type of rock from the bedrock they were sitting on. They had been plucked up and carried here by a glacier from their original location miles away, and left behind when the last of the deep ice melted off about 9,000 years ago. The proper name for them is "erratics," a word I can never remember; it keeps filtering imperfectly into my memory as "mavericks" or "nonconformists"—which is what these rocks really look like, sitting there in their mood of monstrous disarray.

Farther up, a cliff crowding close to the trail was split into vertical slabs by the freezing and thawing of water. One fracture, at least eight feet wide, ran through the outcrop for 200 feet, with rock fragments

Towering over Owens Valley, the eastern flank of the Sierra Nevada forms a wall 55 miles long and rises to 14,494 feet. This awesome escarpment, created partly by the uplift of the Sierra block, partly by the dropping of the Owens Valley, gives evidence that it is still increasing in height: an uplift of more than 13 feet was the cause of an earthquake that devastated the valley in 1872.

strewed along the steep floor of the cleft in a kind of staircase. Near the top of the stair, preserved by shade, was a wind- and water-sculpted monument of snow about 12 feet high, standing alone, touching no walls. These fractures or joints are laced through most of the exposed bedrock of the Sierra, many of them running both vertically and horizontally in a single rock face. In some places the joints are so evenly spaced and close together they create symmetrical blocks that tumble out in time, eventually, giving the mountainside the appearance of a neatly worked quarry.

A quarter of a mile below the lake the trail petered out onto a sloping field of rock, and I dismounted to walk the last piece over rounded slabs made slippery by brown lichen. High above the lake, whose surface was being scratched on this blustery day by gray cats'-paws, the torn skyline of the divide was almost entirely of light-gray granitic rock; but in two places, hanging from the crest like dark tapestries, were remnants of the ancient metamorphic rock that constituted this land before there was a Sierra. And in the rock by the lake's eastern shore was a concise, almost diagrammatic record of the turmoil in the bowels of the earth when the Sierra was being born. The face of one slab was inscribed with a narrow three-layered ribbon of rock—black-white-black—that had been contorted eons ago into four identical waves as steeply concave as those of a Japanese ink drawing of a storm at sea. In the trough of the fourth wave the ribbon broke off abruptly; then, offset some 14 inches, it started again to meander in curves and whorls along the rock—a perfect miniature of the folding and faulting processes that helped to shape these great mountains.

Oddly, this same slab was strewed with small bits of pumice, a porous volcanic rock so light that a piece tossed in Anne Lake floated for some time, until the water seeped into its microscopic pores. The pumice must have come here on the wind, for the nearest possible source was a pair of dormant craters, called the Red Cones, 10 miles away. The volcanic debris must have blown from there millions of years ago, when superheated gases and molten matter burst through the twin fissures in a shower of red-hot rock and ash. Such eruptions—often on a far more terrible scale—have tormented the Sierra for 150 million years, and there is no present sign that they will stop. In fact the lowlands beyond the Red Cones have an unfinished look, as though the earth is still wondering what to do. Hummocks and ridges of hardened lava poke up among the gray sweeps of desert sage. And in the meadows, dark clusters of pitted rock lie carelessly tossed about from recent outbursts whose residue of heat still issues from fumaroles and warm springs in the hills nearby.

There were other vivid signs of earth building in the sweep of the high valley dropping down from Anne Lake. Below the granitic slope a second, much larger lake, Peter Pande, had begun to silt in at the far end, eventually to become a meadow. It is in the nature of such ponds to fill slowly with the detritus of their feeder streams; and one day, where a half-mile stretch of water now glittered, there would be, instead, grass and a scattering of lodgepole pines. Beyond Peter Pande the land plunged into the deep glacial trough of Cascade Valley, whose far wall was embroidered with cataracts formed when the ice mass ground through the main valley and left the side streams hanging a thousand feet or more in the air. And among the heights still farther off was one of the most dramatic illustrations in the whole Sierra of the forces that created this wild country. Three long rockslides, each one touching its neighbor, had spilled from the head of one minor peak whose rock strata were canted at an angle of some 60 degrees. The more distant slide was the deep red-brown color of rock that had been metamorphosed by subterranean heat and pressure, then oxidized when its surface minerals were exposed by erosion; the center slide was bright white, the freshly broken rock from a granitic face; and the nearest slide was the blue black of old volcanic rock. Reining the horses close by these rockslides two days before the Anne Lake trip, a riding companion had said: "See how that granitic rock made its way right up there between the volcanic and metamorphic rock? The rock is standing right on end. In fact, this whole country is standing on end."

This whole country—or at least large portions of it—has been standing on end for about 40 to 45 million years, since the present mountains were thrust up, but the rocks that make up the range have their origins long, long before that. Beginning about 550 million years ago the Sierra region was covered by a succession of seas, alternating with periods of crustal movement that gave rise to mountains. These, in turn, were worn down by erosion. Marine deposits accumulated in layers several miles thick during the periods that the region was under water. Silt from coastal streams and the fine fallout from countless volcanoes also settled in layers thousands of feet thick. Then, in a series of uplifts, powerful contortions of the earth's crust folded and pressed in upon the compacted sediments with enough force to change their chemical makeup so that one day they would show their faces in the High Sierra as the red brown of metamorphic rock or the blue-black mutations of old volcanic debris. While the rocks warped into undulating folds—macrocosms of the wavy pattern on the rock by Anne Lake—other forces within the earth cracked or faulted the strata, sliding enormous blocks of the earth's crust past each other. Rocks that were once adjacent to one another ended up thousands of feet apart. Some of the rocks slid beneath others until very slowly they were pushed up against another, coming to rest at violent angles.

During the agonies of folding and faulting that wracked the area some 95 to 80 million years ago, masses of molten rock—or magma—started to force their way up toward the surface, shouldering aside the existing rock. In places where the earth's crust was weakest, some of the magma burst through to build volcanoes. But most of the magma stopped its rise well below the surface of the earth. There it cooled, hardened and formed what is known as the Sierra Nevada batholith—the enormous granitic mass that is the bedrock of the present-day range. Millions of years later, the batholith and the layers of metamorphic rock that lie over it were slowly uplifted, along with all the rest of the land between the Pacific Coast and the Rockies. This uplift marks the birth of the Sierra as we now know it.

Streams formed in the newly created mountain range, cutting out valleys and steepening the slopes. In the southern and eastern parts of the Sierra, the streams and the rain that spawned them ate away at the old rock cover until the domes and ridges of granitic bedrock emerged to dominate the landscape, and there was little left of the ocean-laid metamorphic rock but isolated massifs like the Kaweah Peaks and the Minarets, or smaller remnants such as the darker rockslides above Cascade Valley. To the north of what is now Yosemite, some of these waterways cut through veins of quartz containing grains and masses of a bright yellow metal whose eroded pieces mingled as pebbles and dust among the stream-bed gravels. Then, between 30 and five million years ago, a sequence of volcanic eruptions buried the northern streams and valleys and all but the tallest peaks under thousands of feet of lava and ash flows.

In a gigantic and protracted movement of the earth that subsided about two million years ago, the entire Sierra was uplifted once again and tilted toward the west. Moist winds rolled up the steepening slopes from the Pacific to drop snow and rain onto the highlands, creating new rivers and rich forest cover on the western flank, but leaving a rain shadow of parched land to the east. Like so many vestiges of youth, this weather pattern and other traits from the Sierra's epoch of growth remained etched upon the character of the mountains.

Today the land that lies to the east of the crest of the Sierra is still a desert, while blizzards continue to howl up the western slope, leaving some of the deepest snow anywhere in North America. During one stretch in 1969 it snowed for 30 days without stop, forcing the Mammoth Mountain ski area in the east-central Sierra to shut down because the snow had buried many of the chair lifts; and in 1906-1907 a record of 73½ feet fell at Tamarack in the central Sierra. The melt from the annual snow cover supplies the ground water for the superb trees of the western-slope forests. The newer rivers born of the great snowpack have long since chewed down and back into the mountains. In the cutting, some of those rivers laid bare the yellow-speckled gravels that had been buried under volcanic debris; and in so doing they condemned all of California to quickened transformation from wilderness to the most populous American state.

On January 24, 1848, a carpenter named James W. Marshall saw golden flecks in the shallows of the American River near a sawmill he had built for an eccentric entrepreneur, Captain John A. Sutter. Marshall sifted an ounce and a half of the yellow stuff from among the sand and pebbles, and rode 30 miles to hand the bright dust to Sutter for testing. It tested out too well for the taste of Sutter, already a rich man whose dream was to maintain a pastoral utopia that would produce fat profits from more genteel ventures such as farming, ranching, real estate and the fur and grain trade.

"At once, and during the night, the curse of the thing burst upon my mind," wrote Sutter. "I saw from the beginning how the end would be, and the next day I had a melancholy ride to the saw-mill." Within a dozen years the recorded population of California had jumped 25-fold from the sparse 15,000 at the time of discovery. Sutter's kingdom had been trampled and the land stolen from him, and even the high fastnesses of the Sierra were being clawed by gold-hungry forty-niners and their successors, the lumbermen and railroad builders.

Yet these latter-day scratchings by man, infected though they might become, were as nothing compared to the overwhelming violence with which nature, having exposed the gold in the old riverbeds, had gone about the penultimate forming of the Sierra. Somewhere between 10 and three million years ago, the apex of the mountains rose above 14,000 feet, the present elevation of the Sierra crest. (continued on page 58)

The Evolution of Yosemite Valley

No one knows just how Yosemite Valley looked during the successive periods of its development over tens of millions of years. The paintings at right, commissioned to accompany a classic 1930 study of the region by François Matthes, are reconstructions of Yosemite's evolution as imagined by two artists who worked closely with the geologist.

The reconstructions show stages of development that came after most of the formative Sierra uplift had been worn away by weathering and stream erosion. Features of the Valley as we know it began to emerge when streams and then glaciers carved the Sierra rock.

1/ In what Matthes calls the broad valley stage, about 50 million years ago, Yosemite forms a wide trough framed by rolling hills less than 1,000 feet high. Through it meanders the Merced River, joined here and there by similar slow-flowing tributaries. Hardwood forests clothe the slopes. The climate is mild and rainy.

2/ The mountain valley stage, seen about 10 million years ago, marks a new period, when the crest of the Sierra began to rise as the whole range tilted westward. In the painting the Merced River, its course accelerated by this tilting, has cut the valley some 800 feet deeper than it had been during its broad valley stage. The climate has become cooler and drier, and as a result the hardwood forests have largely given way to conifers, among them sequoias.

3/ In the canyon stage about three million years ago, Yosemite, raised by the last and greatest Sierra uplift, has almost attained its present-day height. The Merced, transformed by the uplift into a racing torrent, has carved the valley into a canyon about 3,000 feet deep. The approach of the ice age has brought colder winters; the forests are thinning out.

4/ In the major period of glaciation 250,000 to 700,000 years ago, a blanket of ice, striped with dark moraines of rock rubble, almost fills the valley. The summit of Half Dome (top center) pokes up 700 feet above the glacier. But except for the tops of El Capitan and Eagle Peak, ice overrides all the highlands to the north (left).

5/ The ice sheet advances down the valley again. About 25,000 years ago, the Yosemite glacier, a smaller version of the earlier one, has extended only a short distance beyond Bridalveil Fall (bottom right). It has plowed through the valley, quarrying and polishing its walls and sharp cliffs. The climate is more moderate than during the earlier glaciation. Vegetation spreads in the valley beyond the glacier and atop the cliffs.

6/ At the beginning of post-glacial times, about 10,000 years ago, the glacier has melted away, leaving a high terminal moraine that dams up the valley below Bridalveil Fall, creating a broad lake about 800 feet deep. The Merced River is gradually filling in the lake with gravel, sand and silt, thus forming the level floor that Yosemite Valley displays today.

1/ BROAD VALLEY

4/ MAJOR GLACIATION

2/ MOUNTAIN VALLEY

3/ CANYON

5/ LAST GLACIER

6/ EARLY POST-GLACIAL TIME

During this same time several enormous blocks, the biggest at the sites of the Owens Valley and the Lake Tahoe Basin to the north, moved along faults in the bedrock and began to fall in crescendos of sound and power. For most of 10 million years the blocks continued to drop, with some of the most severe eruptions coming within the last 700,000 years. The worst of all came precisely that long ago when enormous quantities of volcanic matter began to spill out of fissures around a high plateau east of the present site of Mammoth Mountain. So much welled out that there was nothing left beneath the plateau to support it, and the entire land mass collapsed inward some 2,000 feet to form the basin of Long Valley.

It is impossible for most of us to comprehend the awful force of these wrenchings that helped create the Sierra. But there was an indication not long after the Civil War when an earthquake split the floor of the Owens Valley in a display that was sheer terror to virtually everyone who lived through it, but which in the great sweep of the Sierra's creation was no more than a single chord in a masterwork. For several hours one night in late March of 1872 severe tremors rumbled through the hills and tore at the earth around the little valley towns, particularly a hamlet called Lone Pine at the foot of the Mount Whitney escarpment. A contemporary account in a local newspaper began with a burst of headlines: "HORRORS! APPALLING TIMES! EARTHQUAKES! AWFUL LOSS OF LIFE! 25 PERSONS KILLED! HOUSES PROSTRATED! LONE PINE! ITS TERRIBLE CONDITION! MOST HEART-RENDING SCENES!"

A 40-acre field sank seven feet, a small lake disappeared and for a brief time the Owens River ran upstream until its bed was dry, the stranded fish flopping on the bare mud. "In the darkness," according to a later account, "people watched cascades of rock roaring down the mountains in monstrous avalanches, throwing out such brilliant trails of sparks that they were assumed to be flows of lava."

Over in Yosemite, about 120 miles from the epicenter of the quake but very much within the scope of its convulsions, John Muir reveled in the primeval glory of it all, having rushed from his cabin at the first tremor to greet this "noble earthquake."

"The shocks were so violent and varied," he wrote, "and succeeded one another so closely, that I had to balance myself carefully in walking as if on the deck of a ship among waves. . . . Suddenly there came a tremendous roar. The Eagle Rock on the south wall, about half a mile up the Valley, gave way and I saw it falling in thousands of great boulders . . . pouring to the Valley floor in a free curve luminous from friction, making a terribly sublime spectacle—an arc of glowing, passionate fire, fifteen hundred feet span. . . . The sound was so tremendously deep and broad and earnest, the whole earth like a living creature seemed to have at last found a voice and to be calling to her sister planets. In trying to tell something of the size of this awful sound it seems to me that if all the thunder of all the storms I had ever heard were condensed into one roar it would not equal this rock-roar."

Besides the rockslides, the greatest scar on the face of the whole Sierra from all this fury and sound was one wistful little breastwork threading across three miles of the Owens Valley floor and rising perhaps 23 feet at its highest point. The Sierra scarp looming over Lone Pine stands almost 500 times as high—a crude measure of the wrenchings that attended its creation.

By tiny fits and grumblings the escarpment is still growing as the crestline of the range climbs through millennial inches and the unstable valley floor quivers with the 20-odd earthquake tremors that send subliminal shock waves through the mountains each year. For the last 300,000 years, however, nothing more violent than a 50-foot slip has occurred. During that period of time, an entirely different force has finished the work of mountain-making by chiseling the heights into spires, by carving and polishing the cliffs and bowls, and by gouging out some of the deepest valleys in all of America. "In the development of these," wrote the indefatigable John Muir, "Nature chose for a tool not the earthquake . . . but tender snow-flowers noiselessly falling through unnumbered centuries."

This was Muir's flossy way of bringing the Sierra glaciers onstage. Most earth scientists of the time—and particularly the pompous Josiah Whitney, leader of the first scientific survey of the Sierra—believed that the latter-day earth shaping had been done by earthquake, rain, wind and stream flow. Dr. Whitney was an important and influential man; the highest mountain in the whole range had been named for him, and he was loudly sure of himself. Especially he was sure that Yosemite Valley had been created by a monstrous collapse of the earth's surface, and then further modified by weather and water. As for the dirty little ice fields still clinging to the shady sides of so many peaks, "It is doubtful whether these residual masses of ice can with propriety be called glaciers; they have no geological significance as such."

Muir thought otherwise. And one day in 1871 he found his proof, while following the course of a rivulet in a basin above the valley.

"Tracing the stream back to the last of its chain of lakelets," he reported, "I noticed a deposit of fine gray mud on the bottom. . . . It looked like the mud worn from a grindstone." The stream carrying the mud issued from the bottom of a mound of rocky debris. Putting two and two together, Muir leaped to the conclusion that he had stumbled onto a glacial site. The mound he took to be a moraine—debris dumped by a glacier at its farthest point of advance. He suspected that the mud was actually microscopic grindings of rock scoured off by moving ice, or what scientists now call glacial flour. Climbing to the top of the mound, Muir "was delighted to see a small but well-characterized glacier swooping down from the gloomy precipices of Black Mountain." Then in best Muir style he recalled having shouted to the winds, "A living glacier!" That ceremony over, he set about studying the several moraines left by the glacier; and the following year he returned to confirm that the frozen body was indeed a living glacier by setting markers at its edge and periodically measuring the movement of the ice.

From this discovery and from later studies, Muir sketched out a pattern of glaciation in the Sierra. Somewhere back in time, he said, the range had been covered by an icecap, part of the vast, frozen sea thought to have inundated much of North America during a single glacial era that 19th Century geologists called the Great Ice Age. According to Muir, the ice sheet had at one point covered the entire Sierra, including its loftiest peaks. Some of them were ground by the moving ice into the shape of domes, and the face of one such eminence was torn off to create Half Dome. Muir also believed that glaciers had gouged out thousands of lakes and deep, steep-walled valleys into which side streams plunged for thousands of feet in the most spectacular set of waterfalls anywhere in the world. Then the whole North American ice field was supposed to have melted back, leaving as its residue in the Sierra little snippets of living ice.

As modern-day geologists have since confirmed, Muir was in large measure correct in his assessment of the role glaciers played in refining the face of the Sierra. But at the time when Muir first published his theories, sophisticated techniques of geologic proof were not available. There was only visual evidence upon which an observer could build a kind of pragmatic logic. And what Muir regarded as proof was not nearly good enough for the likes of crusty old Josiah Whitney, who felt that when he had said, "No glaciers," well then, "no glaciers" is what everyone should jolly well believe. "A more absurd theory was never advanced than that by which it was sought to ascribe to glaciers the sawing out of these vertical walls and the rounding of the domes," he rumbled. "This theory, based on entire ignorance of the whole subject, may be dropped without wasting any more time upon it." Muir, furthermore, was "a mere sheepherder, an ignoramus." So much for the messiah of the Sierra wilderness.

Nor was this blast the only heroic misfire by Whitney in the geologic field. Besides writing off Muir and the glaciers, and creating Yosemite Valley by a phantom earthquake, he was the bombastic victim of one of the most delicious frauds in the history of earth science. In February 1866 a report reached Whitney that an ancient skull, antedating by millions of years any previous human remains found in the Sierra, had been brought up from a mineshaft in the gold town of Cherokee Flat, in Calaveras County. By no coincidence whatever, Whitney had long insisted that the majority of scientists had been wrong in their estimates of the comparatively recent arrival of man, contemporaneous with the mastodon, in these mountains. Now here was the evidence, which Whitney hastened to pass around. "We have the skull at the office," Whitney wrote to his brother. "It is a bona fide find of the greatest interest, all the particulars of which I shall work up with the greatest care." He thereupon worked them up, to the accompaniment of approving nods from the guardians of such bastions of knowledge as Harvard and the *American Journal of Science.*

What Whitney did not know was that the particulars had previously been worked up with care by a bunch of local characters in Cherokee Flat. They had lifted the skull from a display in a doctor's office, had stuffed it into the gravel of the mine, and had then solemnly passed on the news to Whitney of a great anthropological breakthrough. The only security leak in the conspiracy was a poem published at the time by no less than Bret Harte, whose imaginary interview with the so-called Calaveras Skull follows, in part:

> *"Speak, thou awful vestige of the Earth's creation,—*
> *Solitary fragment of remains organic!*
> *Tell the wondrous secret of thy past existence,—*
> *Speak! thou oldest primate!"*
>
> *Even as I gazed, a thrill of the maxilla,*
> *And a lateral movement of the condyloid process,*
> *With post-pliocene sounds of healthy mastication,*
> *Ground the teeth together.*

And, from that imperfect dental exhibition,
Stained with expressed juices of the weed Nicotian,
Came these hollow accents, blent with softer murmurs
Of expectoration;

"Which my name is Powers, and my crust was busted
Falling down a shaft in Calaveras County,
But I'd take it kindly if you'd send the pieces
Home to old Missouri!"

Whitney, as usual, ignored this bit of artful revelation. And Calaveras Man lived on in many corners of the anthropological world until a scientific stake was driven through its heart in the form of several paragraphs of exposé in a learned paper titled *Tertiary Gravels of the Sierra Nevada of California*, published in 1911.

For all Dr. Whitney's stubborn pomposity, however, it would be unfair to judge him in the light of 20th Century knowledge. At the time he was delivering his pronouncements, earth science was in its infancy, and he was not much more wrong than a great many of his contemporaries with a geologic bent; he was only noisier. Even Muir, whose novel glacier theory was much closer to the mark than any other 19th Century explanation of the Sierra's geologic history, erred in thinking that the region had experienced a single, uninterrupted Great Ice Age. Instead, glaciers came and went at least three times, beginning 700,000 years ago. Furthermore, the present Sierra ice fields are not leftovers from prehistory but the younger remnants of a cold cycle called the Little Ice Age that occurred as recently as the 15th to the 19th Centuries. With the exception of Half Dome, which indeed was plucked at by ice, the glacial times had hardly anything to do with shaping the domes. These were made eons before when the upwelling granitic rock cooled in the form of great bulges; and they have kept their shape in a very odd manner. In addition to cracking horizontally and vertically like most rock, these massive domes shed outer layers of stone as a result of repeated heating and cooling. And there is no way of knowing when the rock will have an impulse to shed: a few years ago a ranger riding the ledge trail into Yosemite's Illilouette basin was thrown hundreds of feet to his death when the shelf he was riding on was sloughed off by its mother rock.

Like an understanding of sea-floor spreading and silicon ions, such reversals, corrections and additions to scientific theory probe a great deal deeper into the Sierra's origins than any ordinary wilderness traveler really needs go. And though such an attitude is perhaps irresponsibly antiscientific, I must confess that as just one more such traveler, I am perfectly happy with a concept like a single Great Ice Age. Though I know it has been disproved, its simple logic appeals to me and helps me to understand my Sierra better and thus to love these mountains even more by feeling I know something of both their parts and the sum of them. In the same way, I can even entertain Whitney's notion of a catastrophic collapse at Yosemite with equanimity.

I do not really need to know the exact date of manufacture of the dizzy cliff my horse is skirting; it is enough that the precipice was made by a glacier, and that the mountainside is shining so brightly from the enduring polish left by the ice's passage that the light seems to come from within the earth itself. And I do not really need to know which of three glaciers left scratches on the outcrop so subtle that some of them cannot be seen with the eye, yet can be felt by the soft pads of fingertips drawn across the face of the rock; it is enough that on a warm day I can lean against that scratched rock and dream of the time when the ice was here, and woolly mammoths crossed the frozen river stalked by the saber-toothed tiger and the dire wolf. And I do not need to know the glacial dating of the great bowl in whose clear lake I am fishing; it is enough that the trout are there, and the bowl is so vast a hiker walking away from me gets smaller and smaller until he simply disappears, having reached the vanishing point of his own size in distance. All that is good enough for me.

The Sculptured Rock

From almost anywhere on the rim of Yosemite Valley, a visitor can see a dramatic tableau in what is one of the world's great displays of sculptured granitic rock—the Sierra. The colossal formations that make up the walls of the valley show an incredible variety of contrasting shapes and textures: slab-sided cliffs and slender pinnacles, rounded domes and broad slopes of shattered rock. Granting that erosion works selectively, the visitor still may wonder how such hard granitic rock—granodiorite, quartz monzonite and granite—could have taken on so many different features.

The answer is far from obvious —but a close-up look at several rock surfaces yields a clue: most granitic rock is crosscut by a grid of deep fractures called joints (because they resemble the masonry joints in a stone building). Formed during the course of mountain building, when the molten rock cooled, hardened and shrank, these joints were originally tight. Then cracks developed along them as erosion removed tons of surface rock, exposing portions once deeply buried and causing changes in internal pressure. The spacing of the joints is an important key to Yosemite's varied sculpturing: when the joints are separated by a relatively narrow interval, they weaken the rock and make it more susceptible to wear and breakup than it would be if its joints were farther apart.

During the ice ages, rivers of ice more than 4,500 feet thick bulldozed through Yosemite Valley. The ice plucked, ground and tore pieces of rock, some of them as large as houses, from the walls and floor of the valley along the joints, and dragged them downhill. This process, continuing for thousands of years, gradually deepened and widened the rocky contours of the valley until it acquired its present U-shaped profile.

Domes, the massive, gently rounded structures that dot Yosemite, were once thought to be monoliths— solid, jointless and therefore far stronger than other rock formations found in the valley. But later research indicates that the domes too have joints that are worked on by erosion and glaciers. Even Yosemite's spectacular Half Dome, whose crest rose far above the glaciers, did not escape their sculpting force. The moving ice undercut Half Dome's base and helped to shape its sheer valley-side face.

Although Yosemite's Half Dome looks invulnerable, it is gradually being whittled away. Frost action enlarges and weakens the vertical joints that streak the clifflike face, causing slabs of rock to fall off. The joints visible on Half Dome's curved surfaces also offer points of attack.

The Cracking, Peeling Domes

Though the Sierra's domes are its most durable feature, they are—like all homogeneous rock—subject to a peculiar process of disintegration. The rounded surface of a dome tends to crack and peel off in concentric layers as an onion does. This stripping, called exfoliation, is the result of several factors. One is the changing pressure that occurs within a dome when erosion removes some of its outermost rock. Repeated heating and cooling produce cracks just below and parallel to the surface. Water seeps into such cracks, where it freezes and expands, eventually forcing a thin sheet of rock to loosen and peel off.

In most domes, the surface peels off in layers less than 10 feet thick, though a few formations—among them Yosemite's Royal Arches—display broken layers over 100 feet thick. Each layer that peels off decreases the size of the dome, and the process of exfoliation begins all over again on the newly exposed surface.

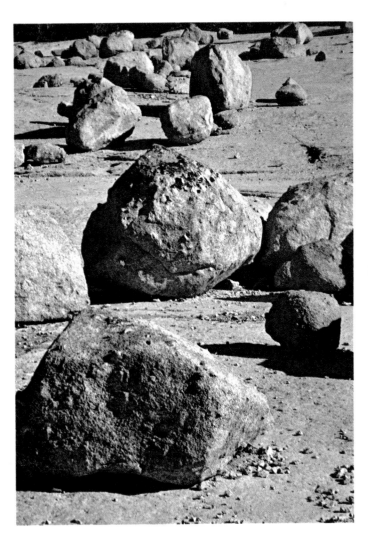

Monuments Marking the Glacier's Wake

The abrasive rubble picked up by glaciers was put down as much as 60 miles away from its point of origin. Among these deposits are the boulders at left, strewn in ones and twos by a melting glacier. Such stray boulders are called erratics. At a loss to explain why they differed from the surrounding rocks, one early theorist suggested that they had been washed from afar by Noah's flood.

Seeded with abrasive sand and rock, glaciers ground broad tracts of exposed granitic bedrock to a high gloss. In the picture at right, a typical example of glacial polishing gleams on a wall above Tuolumne Meadows in a canyon adjoining Yosemite Valley. The dull, rough patches are spots where the rock's glossy surface has weathered and disintegrated. Eventually all of the glacial polish will disappear.

Terraces Carved by Ice and Rain

Ice-age glaciers carved out the valleys of the Sierra by a ripping process called quarrying, which left behind spectacular sculptures like the terrace at left. The terrace began to take shape when some of the ice at the base of the glacier melted. The runoff trickled into the vertical and horizontal joints of the bedrock beneath the glacier, where it froze once again. As the glacier moved on downhill, blocks surrounded by ice-filled joints were yanked out of the bedrock. By quarrying millions of individual blocks and slabs, the glacier slowly cut downward through hundreds of feet of rock.

This gently sloping terrace has a strikingly different configuration and texture from the one at left, despite the fact that they are of the same age and composition. Grade and gravity account for the differences. On the easy incline, a rock pried loose by frost action is more likely to remain in place than to roll downhill to the bottom of the terrace. Under the attack of rain, melting snow and ice, the surface of the rock crumbles bit by tiny bit, and eventually becomes roughened and pitted. The same weathering process wears away any sharp edges and produces rounded contours. By contrast, rocks loosened from the steep terrace tend to tumble off, giving the terrace a smooth face of freshly exposed, relatively unweathered rock.

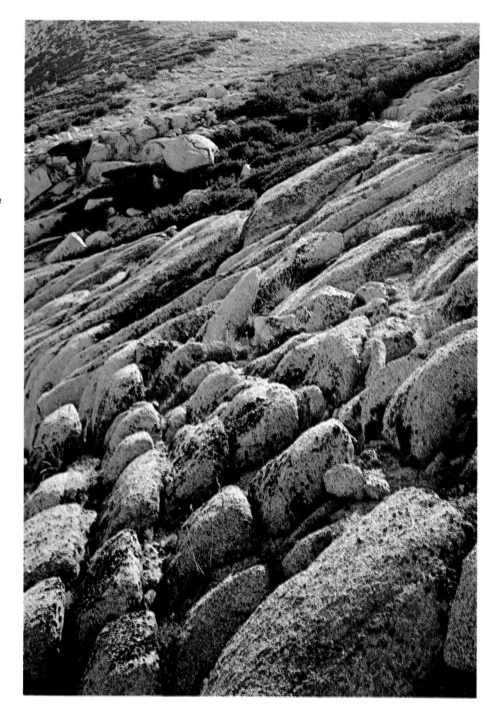

3/ The Range of Light

The impression is one of grandeur, but at the same time of desolation—the dark pines, the light granite, the absence of all sounds except the sighing of the wind through the pines...

W. H. BREWER/ *UP AND DOWN CALIFORNIA IN 1860-1864*

It is noon. And my horse stands, belly heaving from the morning climb, at the crest of Duck Pass, gateway between the bustling settlement of Mammoth Lakes on the eastern slope and the 503,258-acre John Muir Wilderness. Never among any mountains, nor perhaps anywhere on earth, have I seen a richness of color to match the spectrum along this trail. The natural tones range from the white of tiny snow fields tucked into shaded gullies on peaks above the lake to the blue black of ancient volcanic outcroppings among the granitic bedrock. At this moment Duck Lake just below me is most dramatic. It measures some 258 acres on the surface, is 300 feet deep, and its color is the same perfect blue of the ocean that I have seen in Davis Strait between the Baffin Island and Greenland, and in the Pacific where the trade winds roll down to Hawaii. Only very deep water takes on this hue, and the lake's bottom contours, scooped out by a glacier, are indeed so profound that the water absorbs every color in the spectrum but the blue.

Beyond the meadow the water vanishes in a drought-shriveled cascade; but from the look of the land below, the symphony of Sierra color will continue all day as our pathway drops through switchbacks and long undulations toward the valley campground by Fish Creek. Muir himself was so dazzled by the Sierra's brilliant tones, its mirror lakes and shining rocks that he called these mountains the Range of Light. There is another name, an Indian word, that I like better: Inyo, the Dwelling Place of a Great Spirit. The Paiutes, who roamed the eastern foothills and valleys until the white man came, first gave the word to the mountains east of the Owens Valley, and now this section up to the crest of the Sierra bears it as well, as part of the Inyo National Forest. Here dwells Numunana, the People Father, with whom the Paiutes spoke as they traveled the wilderness. They spoke, too, with the guardian powers that are within all the rocks, the snow, the trees and wild things. They drew strength from these powers, and from the wind, too, and from the blue desert haze that often hangs over the valley.

No part of the Sierra belongs to the Paiutes now; but the rightful name for this land of austere beauty will always be Inyo, for the high country remains the dwelling place of a great spirit. Among these granitic crests there is an aura of exhilaration, of awe and fulfillment. To one who knows the Sierra well and comes back to the high country after having been away for a time, there is, too, the joyous rush of recognition that strikes a sailor walking the streets of a city when a sudden turn of wind brings him the sea air. Seeing Inyo now bathed in the clearest light of noon, I feel once more the wish that no one had ever been in this wilderness before. At least, no white man.

Yet along the approaches to the wild country the presence of 20th Century white man has been pervasive. On the way up this morning we passed dozens of people, some of them hunkered down beside lakes and streams to fish or snooze, others sifting along the trail with us. Among the walkers was a scattering of pale-skinned city couples, the men with notably smooth faces and combed hair, the women in slacks and cardigan sweaters thrown over T-shirts. They have headed back to the parking lots at the Mammoth Lakes roadhead, having taken their little nibble of the Sierra. And although this is their land as much as ours, it is hard not to feel intruded upon by them.

There has also been a sense of intrusion from the obvious management of the trail itself. Rangers from the U.S. Forest Service, which administers this sector of the Sierra, have carried aside all loose rocks. At short intervals small logs called water bars have been embedded slantwise in the path to lead off snowmelt and rain so the trail does not erode as a sluiceway. At longer intervals but with insistent frequency, small wooden signs tell the traveler exactly where he is (Duck Lake Trail, Reds Meadow 9 miles; John Muir Trail 5 miles; Purple Lake 8 miles), with arrows pointing down the various branch trails.

About an hour back we passed an even bigger sign announcing the border of the Muir Wilderness: WELCOME TO THE BACK COUNTRY, ENJOY IT,

PRESERVE IT. Surely, we felt, from here on the human presence would be less noticeable.

Immediately we encountered more people. However they were a different sort, and to them, we were the intruders. Down from the last pitch to Duck Pass came two young men, strong, tanned, unshaven, one with his hair pulled back by a bandanna. They were backpackers, and from the look of them they had been out a week, their sunburned legs bared by old shorts and their feet laced into dusty hiker's boots. Forest Service rules require backpackers to give way on the trail to horses. Silently the two men half stepped, half stumbled into a small gully, a look of harsh impatience in their eyes. (Backpackers do not like horses, which chew up the trail with their iron shoes and leave their droppings everywhere—a pollution, says the hiker, of the natural environment.)

The two young men near Duck Pass said nothing at all as we rode by. And though they looked unhappy with us, we were relieved, in certain ways, to see them. Their shaggy, weathered appearance contrasted sharply with that of the people on the lower trails, promising wilder land ahead and suggesting a reassuring image of the wilderness as a target with concentric rings, each having its own character and denizens. The bull's-eye is the pure wild—such places as Anne Lake on the heights beyond Fish Creek, or Simpson Meadow in Kings Canyon, or the Lake Italy Basin, lying below the 13,000-foot heights of Mounts Hilgard and Abbot. Surrounding such bull's-eyes are lesser degrees of wildness, from the barest high trails and spartan bivouacs to the manicured paths lower down. The outer ring is the roadhead with its parking lots and managed campgrounds, its bungalows and rental rowboats, all reachable by auto-borne day trippers.

Now, as our horse party crests Duck Pass, we are moving into the second ring of the target, closer to the heart of Inyo. And we notice that on this day the spirit of the mountain seems unsettled, for he is speaking in a tone very different from summer's gentle whispers. Today the spirit is letting us know it is his pleasure to change the season, to change the look of the land. And his warning shout comes rushing heavily through the constriction of the pass, tearing at the stunted mattings of whitebark pine that are the only vestiges of trees to survive here at timber line. The air has a touch of dampness to it, and the wind has bent the wisps of clouds capping the tallest crags into convex curves; their shape is a sign of the celebrated Sierra wave, the high-rising air current that glider pilots the world over come to ride—and announces, too, a deep mutation in the mountain weather.

We have chosen to ignore the warning voice, moving on into the back country, though each of us knows that winter is poised to sweep down from the north, and tonight's dry campground may by morning be a whitened mess of wet saddles, buried food stores and ice-stiffened cinch ropes. The plants and wild creatures of the mountain have heard the voice, too, but they are heeding its message in ways that their genes have dictated over unending centuries. In damp gullies below us the willow shrubs have gone to seed that will soon be carried on the wind by tufts of feathery white fibers to fresh ground, where they will germinate after the snow has come and gone. Along the draws much lower down, the aspen leaves are purest gold from the nightly frosts that have ended the growing season's production of green chlorophyll, so the leaves show only their yellow pigments before they drop to the ground. At trail's edge, mint-smelling pennyroyal blossoms have turned to brown crumbles as the plant dies back and remains dormant until next year's short growth burst.

A tiny alpine chipmunk has left a neat pile of pine-cone husks on a rock where it has been separating out the seeds to bury in pugholes—tiny storage pits—spotted around the terrain. But it will never eat them, for at our horses' approach the chipmunk skitters over a rise in the open ground and a Cooper hawk, which has been cruising on the buffeting wind, starts downward in scalloped swoops. The denouement is not visible, but I would be reluctant to bet on the chipmunk.

A wiser creature, the pika, keeps hidden inside the entrance to its rocky den, showing no part of itself but making a nasal complaint at our interruption of the last days of preparation for winter. A fist-sized ball of fat and gray-brown fur, the pika is closely related to the rabbit. During the warm weeks just ending, it has gathered bits of grass and plant stems and set them to cure in tiny piles like hay in the sun before storing them as winter forage. Today the pika is nearly ready to call it a season and go to ground under sheltered ledges in the debris of a rockslide, where it will spend the snow time nibbling on the cubic yard of hay it has hidden there.

Unlike the horse party clattering across its habitat, the pika came to the Sierra crest with the basic design for high-country living. It is really an arctic species that migrated here with the glaciers and was marooned on these cold islands of high altitude when the ice receded. Some of the plants, too, have arctic origins that imbued them with the ability to survive in timber line's bitter climate. The green and white splash of saxifrage beneath a rock overhang as we start down toward the lake is identical to a saxifrage that grows at sea level on Devon Island inside the Arctic Circle.

But to the saxifrage, life in the High Sierra is not very good, and in some ways the plant might have been better off if it had stayed home on Devon Island. There it would have just as long a growing season as the 40-odd days it will likely have to settle for here next summer, if the coming winter is as long and hard as is possible in these areas. And there it would not have to endure mid-July snow flurries or the 80° heat of a Sierra summer afternoon. Still the saxifrage has managed to make an accommodation to the Sierra's demanding range of temperature and wind by putting down its roots in damp, shaded places where it can survive the August heat. And it has made an accommodation with the short growing season by staying small: the stem measures only two to four inches, a height that can be reached quickly, and that can withstand fierce winds far better than that of the larger-sized specimens found in gentler climates.

Though such accommodations are so logical as to seem almost cozy, none of these vegetal dwarfs really has a pleasant time of it. "Up here in these higher altitudes," explains one of my riding companions, whose devotion has been the ecology of the High Sierra, "you're looking not at the plants and trees that are happy here, but the ones that are less un-happy." By this theory of environmental negativism none of the hunched and often homely alpine growths is at home in the lonely reaches of timber line and above; yet by reluctant necessity they have worked out their marginal modus vivendi in surroundings that would kill off any lush lowland species.

A tree like the whitebark pine grows along the ground instead of reaching upward into the shrieking wind. Its tough, supple branches are so closely matted that they offer a snug shelter for any hiker or coyote or bighorn sheep that is wise enough to crawl down into them during a mountain storm. During the short summer the tree may restrict its growth to no more than an eighth of an inch, and a limb the thickness of a soda straw can be as much as 75 years old. Thus the whitebark survives at these high altitudes. Yet if a whitebark attempts to move down the slope, it cannot compete with the bigger, handsomer conifers that themselves are unable to survive in the harsh world farther up.

When our horses reach the final switchbacks down to Duck Lake, the whitebark in fact concedes the ground to lodgepole pines scattered in open stands and to spires of blue-green hemlock. The dwarf flowers, too, give way to the taller yarrow and wild onion, each one browned by fall, and to heather and Indian paintbrush whose seasonal red has managed to survive the frost. Down at the lake a meadow bordering the outlet stream shows signs of still another change in the look of things. Every grassy corner and every grove of trees contain a rubble of fire-scarred rocks left in years past by weekend campers who habitually stayed here for the night, having reached the limit of a comfortable one-day hike from the roadhead back at Mammoth Lakes. "People tend to bunch up at imaginary boundary points like that," a ranger had told us in some disgust, "and it makes a mess." It surely does, and the U.S. Forest Service has tried to combat it by restricting the number of both hikers and campsites in the vicinity. Campers now must bring portable stoves for cooking at sites where campfires are prohibited.

Where the meadow meets the lake, a weir of rock with the weathered wooden slats of a fish barrier in the middle stretches across the mouth of the outlet stream. It was put there by the California Department of Fish and Game, custodian of the creatures in this wilderness (animals and fish in most national forests are managed by state agencies). The barrier's purpose was to maintain a balance of fish life the department itself had created in waters that had been barren. In ages past this lake and most of the other 2,000 lakes and ponds in the Sierra were formed by glaciers gouging out depressions that were filled with rain water and snow melt. Native rainbow trout in the waters at lower altitude were unable to make their way to the high lakes, although they were able to reach such valley waters as Fish Creek. There, as the name implies, they thrive.

Beginning about 1870 various anglers, and later the Fish and Game people, sprinkled rainbow and brook trout around the high lakes. They also transplanted some golden trout from the southern Sierra. And they built barriers and weirs to keep everything in its new habitat. Whereupon the fish, in the manner of most wild things, began to behave in all sorts of ways that no one had anticipated.

Some of the goldens mated with their close cousins, the rainbows, to spawn a hybrid species; and the rest of the goldens fell victim to the predaceous tendencies of the aggressive brook trout, a species that tends to eat its neighbors rather than breed with them. Once the fish had finished mating or murdering, however, few of them really prospered. For a lake in the High Sierra, like the land itself, does not provide enough nourishment to support a strong food chain. There are too few algae to feed many crustaceans and other crawly things, which are thus too sparse to fatten up the trout. But in the years following World War II the Department of Fish and Game planted trout in virtually every food-poor High Sierra puddle big enough to hit with an airdrop of hatchery fingerlings. Naturally most of the trout stayed hungry. "Some of these mountain fish are so starved they grab at anything that even looks like food," says a Montana ranchwife with a saddlebag full of trout flies and spinning gear. The trout also tend to stay small. A pond not far from Duck Lake once yielded up a 20-year-old brook trout measuring less than eight inches and weighing only a quarter of a pound (with decent food a brook trout can grow a pound a year).

In a burst of experimentation designed to provide bigger fish rather than just busy fishing, the department introduced into Duck Lake the Kamloops, a salmonlike strain of rainbow native to British Columbia. The Kamloops have got on handsomely, growing up to three pounds on a diet of available crustaceans supplemented by the Sierra's terrestrial insect life, which prospers in the wet shore grass through spring and summer but which, mercifully for our particular party, expires with the coming of heavy frost.

The sum total of the Department of Fish and Game's busy hand, the planted species and the weirs and barriers, is unquestionably good fishing. In the broader sense it might be called good recreational planning for the increasingly heavy numbers of people who come into the Sierra. I would call it nothing of the kind, for it raises a disturbing question: should there be all this fiddling in a wild preserve that Congress has said must retain "its primeval character ... with the imprint of man's work substantially unnoticeable"?

At least one of my mountain companions thinks not. "Even some of our Fish and Game biologists are beginning to feel that the problems we've got up here are entirely man-caused," she says. "Our fish populations had reached equilibrium. But we kept putting our grubby fingers in there, overexploiting, letting one species take over from another. It's improper land use."

I agree with the woman. As I have told you before, this is my Sierra. I know just how the place should be run.

On the other hand our horse packer and guide, a devout angler, cannot believe anyone could be so stupid as to think as I do. He likes his lakes full of trout and is dead set against pulling out the weirs. "All the trout would swim over the falls," he says, "and we'd lose them." He speaks with the blunt conviction of a lifetime outdoorsman. He is, in

Seeming to grow from naked rock, a Sierra juniper clings to an exposed slope, its gaunt branches pushed to one side by the unrelenting force of the wind. Its plant neighbors growing on higher ridges are dwarfed and gnarled by steady 60-mile-an-hour gales.

fact, a third-generation Californian whose great-grandfather ran fire-arms and supplies to the Sierra hideaway of two antiestablishment gun-slingers in the 19th Century. The strain of hard-nosed independence is still strong in the family blood, and the packer is profanely certain the Sierra is his. He resents the Forest Service's effort to instill a "no-trace" ethic on wilderness visitors by dismantling permanent fireplaces and encouraging the use of portable stoves. His personal wilderness philosophy is unabashedly selfish—to restrict casual visitors to developed campsites, where they can "concentrate the mess" while leaving the rest of the Sierra to more appreciative types like himself.

With his diatribe completed, he unhitches the lead ropes to let the horses and mules graze awhile, and plops down against a tree to begin stuffing his mouth with massive hunks of sandwich. The rest of us dismount to chew on our lunch and wash it down with lake water. Afterward I fold my jacket and hat against a boulder away from the wind, scooch my back in the sand and pine cones to make a smooth depression, and doze as the low chuckling of the stream and the soughing of the midday wind play a gentle duet around me.

I awaken to find the packer sitting next to me. And I ask him why, with all the water and grass and good brush cover along the trails, we have not seen a single deer since we came into the wilderness. He laughs and tells me I am in too much of a hurry. Whenever people come into the wilderness, he says, they are greedy for a quick look at the biggest and best of the wildlife. Yet almost half of all Sierra visitors never see anything bigger than a chipmunk. For wilderness is not a condensable experience wherein the creatures scurry by in an enchanting parade, performing cute little rituals as they might in a Disney fantasy. The larger animals, particularly the predators, make their living by staying out of sight as much as possible, both from simple native caution and from having been shot at for over a century.

The coyote of the Sierra has been a career target for sheep ranchers, particularly in the foothills where stockmen fire away at any wild dog unwise enough to show its face. Therefore the coyote tries not to. The mountain lion, more lethal as a predator and therefore deeply disliked by stockmen, is of an even more private persuasion. The deer, too, are man-shy—that is to say, gun-shy—and it takes patience, luck and a practiced eye to see them with any regularity. In a recent survey a group of casual hunters reported that they spotted seven deer over a two-day period in an area where a trained naturalist had counted 60. Since our own counts thus far have been zero, the packer takes care to explain where the deer might be if any of us would learn how to pay attention.

"See that up there by the pass?" he asks, pointing to a little hanging meadow southwest of the notch we came over this morning. His finger indicates a faint zigzag thread of trail traced across the open ground. He explains that the trail was not made by people. Rather it is the main deer migration route out of the summer feeding ground in the valley of the Fish Creek region. Through these fall days the deer have stayed down in the moist, protected bottoms, fattening on aspen and willow and other tender shoots. When dustings of snow begin to blow in, they will become restless. Then with the first heavy blizzard they will start out over the pass and down Mammoth Creek to their winter range in the eastern lowlands. It is still too warm for them to begin moving, the packer says. Nevertheless, if we look sharp, tonight along the creek, or tomorrow morning in the meadows, we may see a few.

When we remount, the horses turn reflexively back toward the pass, having been heavily programed to do so by a lifetime of day rides out of the Mammoth stables. They are not at all pleased to be thumped and reined around until they are pointing the other way. They bridle at the signposted junction where the Duck Lake Trail runs into the Muir Trail, making it altogether clear that they may yet decide to go home for the night. During the ensuing 20 minutes or so, there is a shared and stubborn uncertainty between horse and rider about who is *numero uno*. Naturally I make every outward sign it will be me. But secretly, like any dude in his bright new Levi's, I am not at all convinced. Nor, for that matter, is my horse. We have been on the trail only one day, and I am very conscious of being too fresh from the city myself, too soft of hand and foot, and not a little uncertain of the land ahead.

In addition to these qualms of the spirit, a very real physical crisis has arisen from the conformation of the horse. Whereas the legs of a movie cowboy seem to drop comfortably down into his stirrups, the legs of an ordinary mortal are forced outward by the horse's rib cage and then pulled inward by the slant of the dangling irons. For a middle-aged rider this causes some exquisite agony in the thighs. During the morning it has helped—though not much—to dismount periodically and walk along beside the horse, thus preventing obsolescent muscles and ligaments from freezing altogether in the pain of unfamiliar positions. Gradually, however, like the whitebark on the mountain, horse and rider are reaching an accommodation.

Not a moment too soon. Suddenly, though the symphony of color still plays around us and the air has warmed to early afternoon, the character of the trip changes frighteningly. Up to this point we have been on wide, gradual trails, on lake shores and near beaten-down campgrounds. We have been safe, cruising rather than adventuring. Now, however, we are threading our way along the side of a chasm and have just crossed an avalanche gully bisecting the trail. The Sierra rock is everywhere—not just grandly in the distance but very much underfoot in loose rocks and ahead in slick, slanted slabs the horses must negotiate. Around the next bend the land below the trail disappears altogether, and through a break in the treetops I can see just under my right boot a gorge so deep and steep-sided that the bottom is not yet visible, even here from the edge.

A little giddy from the altitude, I have slipped my boots away from the stirrups so as to be able to bail out quickly if the horse makes a significant misstep. This precaution turns out to be silly, since all the pack-train animals are beautifully steady and every bit as interested in survival as their riders. Nevertheless, the fear of heights is a powerful force, and like most lowlanders I will never conquer the habit of leaning slightly toward the mountain at such places, a practice that visibly irritates any horse since it pulls him off balance.

At this unhappy moment, with my psyche wrapped in a moist blanket of acrophobia, a pair of jet fighters from nearby Edwards Air Force Base blasts close overhead, splitting the air with their thunderous whistle. I shorten the reins and set my feet back into the stirrups to hold the horse from shying. But when the supersonic boom comes he does not even quiver. He has been through this mountain cleft so often, with the stunting pilots roaring in just beyond the treetops, that he no longer notices. Yet I cannot adjust as well as the horse. Mingled with plain fright is a surge of anger; the sound of the jets is terrible, the screaming voice of war, and it has no place in the wilderness. No place on earth, really, but surely no place here, where people come to be at peace with the earth and with themselves.

The trail takes a turn away from the canyon and onto a 50-degree sloped hillside spotted with timber. Just below us is the first juniper I have seen on this trail, a stunted, wonderfully ugly brute of a tree that seems totally unlike its slender garden-variety relative cultivated on New England lawns. The massive cinnamon-colored trunk of this Sierra juniper, like so many others near timber line, is perhaps four or five feet thick, with the top blasted off about 20 feet up by wind or lightning and the branches streaming off to leeward from the prevailing westerlies. It looks, in all, like an unfinished window display whose top section and other branches never arrived for assembly. Yet there is about it an enduring quality, a homely strength that suggests many seasons and many lives will come and go before this juniper is done.

As if in confirmation, the juniper's bulk rises at the very edge of an avenue of smaller lodgepole pines whose own trunks are broken off eight or nine feet above the ground—the level at which winter avalanches have roared over the deep snowpack, destroying everything tall enough to poke above the surface. Among the tall stumps a rumpling of green shrubs has sprouted, as they typically do along avalanche tracks where the overshading trees have been destroyed and the soil stirred up to create a more hospitable seedbed.

The trail descends rapidly now, along the Purple Lake outlet and down toward Fish Creek in the ultimate valley. The soil all along the slope has had only the barest sprinklings of summer rain to bring life to it. This is typical of the eastern part of the Sierra, where the parched earth supports a more modest race of growing things than does the wetter western region. Certain pines, however, are fond of the crumbly, quick-draining mineral soil. In the higher reaches, the lodgepoles hog the best seedbeds by casting an inhibiting shade and by dropping tannin- and resin-bearing needles and cones that virtually prevent anything else from growing. "A high-altitude desert," the packer calls it. And indeed there the forest floor is bare of everything but a thin litter of cones and needles, looking almost as though it had been cleared and raked. But here below the 9,700-foot level, where the slopes begin to ease toward the valley, the earth holds its moisture better. In fact, the entire climate is measurably milder. The peaks shield the trees and plants from the tearing wind, and for each thousand feet of descent the temperature has risen about 3°, warming the middle-elevation flora so it can grow more profusely.

Although lodgepoles continue to poke up along the trail, the dominant tree is now the Jeffrey pine, a handsome giant of 100 feet and more whose coarse brown bark cracks with the tree's growth into four- or six-sided plates like the skin of an alligator. The bark of one Jeffrey shows a yellow rip exposing a panel of sap-beaded wood, the wound measuring some two feet across and running 20 feet down the trunk to the ground. Lightning hit this tree two summers ago, condemning it to a slow death that has already denuded its upper branches and turned the long silky needles a dry brown. The root but- (continued on page 86)

Patterns of Bark— the Trees' Signatures

From a distance, the trees that forest the Sierra at middle altitude seem uniform: stand after stand of hardy cone-bearing evergreens. Although each species of coniferous tree, when seen close up, has its own definite characteristics (of size, color, shape of cones and needles), the most obvious clue to identity is the tree's protective sheath, its bark.

Between the bark and the wood of a tree is sandwiched a single layer of cells called the cambium. As the cambium cells divide, they create a new layer of wood on the inside and a new layer of bark on the outside. The appearance of the bark often changes as the tree grows older.

The photographs on these two pages show barks of the seven conifers that are common to the Sierra. Three major characteristics distinguish the barks of the various species from one another:

□ Color, determined by the bark's chemical composition, ranges from the purplish red-brown of the giant sequoia to the yellow brown of the ponderosa pine.

□ Pattern varies from the small rectangular blocks that cover the Western white pine to the irregular plates of the ponderosa pine, which look like three-dimensional jigsaw-puzzle pieces.

□ Texture may be rough and ridgy as on the red fir; thick, fibrous and fluted as on the giant sequoia; or relatively smooth, like the finely scaled bark of the lodgepole pine.

SEQUOIA

PONDEROSA PINE (YELLOW PINE)

JEFFREY PINE

WESTERN WHITE PINE

LODGEPOLE PINE

RED FIR

SUGAR PINE

tresses are charred, and vestiges of a ground fire reach out to a radius of about 30 feet, where the fire spent itself, having come to bare soil at the outer edge of the Jeffrey's needle fall.

Such minor lightning fires are common through the High Sierra in late summer and fall; in this very district they occur anywhere from 15 to 120 times in a single year. They are, in fact, as much a part of the natural ecology as the sun and rain. And in some areas at elevations above 8,000 feet the rangers no longer try to put them out, having finally embraced a bit of wisdom any Indian could have shared with them 100 years ago: regular small fires may be healthy for a woodland. They creep around eating up dead underbrush and other forest litter. They clear the ground for new sprouts of underbrush the deer can feed on and for nut-bearing bushes to nourish the smaller animals. More important, they open up patches of forest and let in life-giving sunlight. The giant sequoias and Jeffreys can best seed themselves in ground exposed to light by a providential fire. And one tree, the knobcone pine, cannot sprout at all until the heat of a fire cooks open the cones to let the seeds drop out.

Beyond the small burn the forest floor has a green matting of chaparral, a mixture of shrubby plants common in the dry regions of the Sierra and the adjacent California valleys. About half of it here is buckbrush, a gray-green bush with fragrant leaves and shoots that are a favorite browse for the deer herds. Peering into one thicket I have a wistful hope that any moment, if I look in just the right place, a doe may come slipping through with her hopping, stiff-legged gait. But not today.

The remainder of the undergrowth is manzanita, whose sweet berries and tangle of tough branches provide a safe and profitable foraging ground for rodents and small birds. Manzanita is Spanish for "little apple," after the ruddy-skinned apple-shaped beads of fruit that sprout among the bright green leaves. As we ride along, a scurry of chipmunks and ground squirrels is busy feeding on remnants of the fall-dried fruit, while black-headed juncos flutter among the branches looking for any berry that might not yet have fallen. "The junco," explains one of my companions, "is the most abundant of all our Sierra creatures. And," she adds with scientific solemnity, "the most successful therefore." Being basically nonscientific, I tend to equate success in wild animals not with numbers but with regal presence. And I am therefore much more impressed by a flight of five mountain quail that flashes up in a flutter of blue gray, the dark crest of one cock sweeping back proudly.

It is past 5 when we finally dismount at our campground in a grove of pines and turn out the pack animals in hobbles for the night. The center of the camp is at a sharp bend in the winding course of Fish Creek. Upstream a flat meadow becomes a marshy catch basin for Fish Creek's overflow. Early one season the packer caught a trout by casting into a puddle right in the middle of fresh green grass. In fall, however, the sumps are gray-brown circles of parched mud, and the minor watercourses leading into the creek have become bright pathways of rounded pebbles. The grass is dry, and it looks invitingly soft in the late afternoon sun, a tempting place to lay a sleeping bag. But we will pitch our tents in the grove where the ground is a foot or two higher and free of the evening damp that rises from the meadow to chill a sleeper even in this dry season.

As we walk down to the stream to take up water for the evening meal, a rainbow trout flashes away, and we can see two or three brook trout holding under a log in one of the stills. The packer and I set up our fly rods and make a cursory pass at several pools. But it is quickly growing dark, and the fishing is a formal gesture on our part just to certify that we are now firmly entrenched in the wilderness.

Soon we have generated a fire beneath a pot of stew that, while unquestionably nourishing, has the specific gravity of a sash weight. Nevertheless it fills an enormous gap in the stomach. After dinner, while we are climbing into long underwear and ski parkas against the fast-coming night cold, a full moon rises, etching the treetops' silhouettes against the brilliant glow of granitic ridges, and keeping the Sierra alive with color even into the night. We have heaped the fire with pine knots that burn with bright fragrance from their impregnations of pitch. My tent door faces the fire, whose reflections and shadows run in swift waves along the tent roof. They are the last things I see before dropping into a deep and perfect sleep to awaken to a clear morning, the fire crackling afresh beneath the coffeepot, and the horses and mules rolling in the meadow as the sun moves down the west wall of the valley to reach into our campground.

A Continent on a Mountain

PHOTOGRAPHS BY SONJA BULLATY AND ANGELO LOMEO

The distance from Sonora in northern Mexico to arctic Canada is 2,500 miles. A traveler making this long northward march would encounter a remarkable range of vegetation, from the low, stubborn shrubs of the arid south, through the luxuriant forests of northern America, to the small, quick-growing plants that survive above the Arctic Circle. But such a journey on foot would take the traveler perhaps half a year.

The same plant life can be seen in a fraction of the time on the western slopes of the Sierra Nevada. Each 1,000 feet a hiker climbs corresponds roughly to a northward advance of 300 miles. As he ascends, he traverses separate realms where the conditions and forms of life are similar to those found en route from Mexico to the Arctic. These belts of mountainside vegetation, five in all, are called climatic life zones, each named after the continental region it ecologically resembles.

Climatic life zones are generally determined by altitude, but several other factors are involved: amount of moisture, kind of soil, exposure to sun and wind. Plants climb higher on southward-facing slopes, which receive up to three times more sunlight than northern slopes.

No single plant is an infallible indicator of a particular climatic life zone, since some plants flourish in two or more zones. But as conditions change with elevation, one kind of plant life replaces another in a succession of plant types distinct enough to be broadly recognized.

In the Sierra the journey begins in the foothills—the Upper Sonoran Zone. Here clumps of scrub oak give some relief from the glare of the hot sun on dry hillsides. The traveler senses a change when passing into the Transition Zone at an altitude of several thousand feet, where forests of ponderosa and sugar pines scent the air. At still-higher altitudes these trees give way to the red fir and the lodgepole pines of the Canadian Zone's forests. When the climate becomes cold and windy, and only scraggly species of pine dot a rocky landscape, the traveler is in the Hudsonian Zone, named after the Hudson Bay area of Canada.

Finally, in the treeless Arctic-Alpine Zone, the traveler stands amid desolate vistas of rock broken only by occasional dwarf plants. Here the delicate pink rockfringe huddles for shelter behind a rock—precisely as it does in the Arctic, 2,000 miles away.

This single photograph, taken in the Mount Stewart area, displays all five climatic life zones of the western Sierra slope. The angle of view and the distortion of the lens have condensed distance and perspective: the actual boundaries of the zones are separated by several thousand feet.

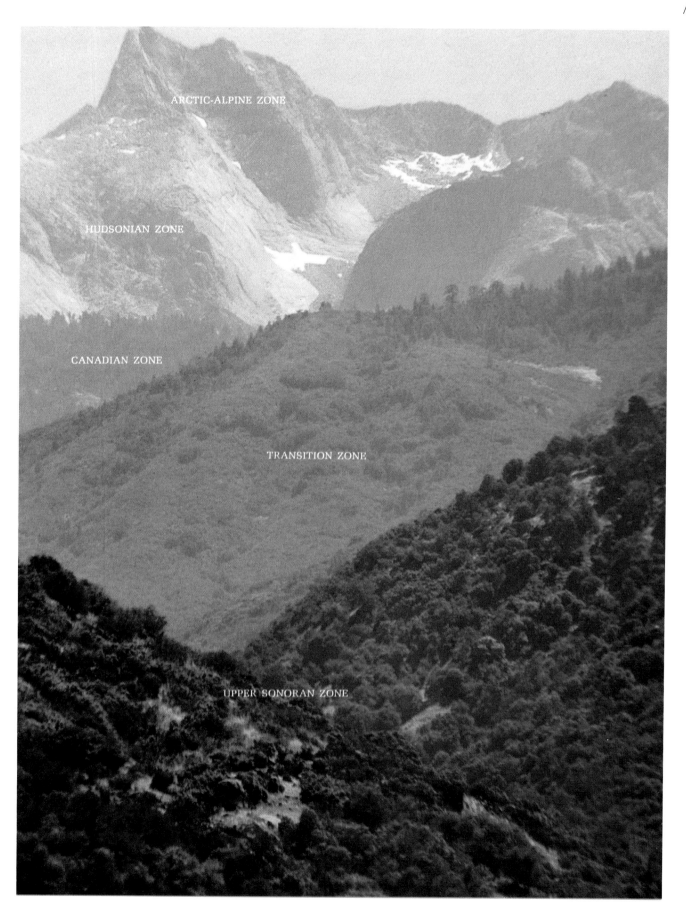

Upper Sonoran Zone: Life in a Dry Climate

Life is not easy for the plants that grow on the sun-baked Sierran foothills at 500 to 2,000 feet. After the March rains the sun burns down until well into October, parching the earth. The rains return in November, but they are meager. There is little snow to soak the ground as it melts.

In this zone, two distinct plant communities thrive: woodland and chaparral. Found on the southern slopes of the foothills, chaparral is a dense thicket composed of several different kinds of shrubby plants, ranging from five to eight feet tall.

On north-facing slopes, and in spots where the soil retains more summer moisture, smooth grass and sparse, rounded clusters of trees give the hills a groomed, parklike appearance. Live oaks, which keep their foliage year round, offer shade; sycamores occasionally mingle with the oaks. Another distinctive tree of the zone—and the first conifer encountered on the western mountain slope—is the digger pine. Its thin, gray needles and widely spaced branches provide little shade.

This ascetic zone knows one moment of exuberance. Beginning in the lower meadows during March and reaching higher levels by April, there is a profusion of tiny wild flowers (opposite and overleaf). It is only a brief extravagance: the flowers will wither by the end of May. A lone exception, standing through June, is the tall farewell-to-spring (bottom right).

LIVE OAK AND (RIGHT) CALIFORNIA SYCAMORE

OWL CLOVER

FIESTA FLOWER

FAREWELL-TO-SPRING

MINER'S LETTUCE

CALIFORNIA POPPY

VIOLET

LACEPOD, OR FRINGEPOD

FIVE-SPOT

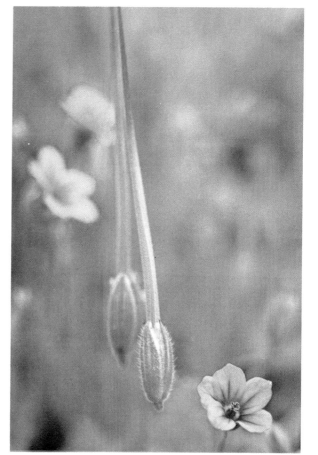

FILAREE

The Transition Zone: A Place of Gentle Weather

A climate that is hospitably temperate identifies the Transition Zone, which begins at an altitude of 2,000 feet and on some south-facing slopes extends to 9,000 feet. Winters are cool and snowy, supplying up to 80 inches of precipitation. During the warm summers there is little rain, but fogs supply ample moisture.

These benign conditions have nurtured a magnificent forest, heavily populated by ponderosa pine. The naturalist John Muir, who loved the sound of wind blowing through the ponderosas, described specimens 200 feet tall with cones as big as pineapples. But more often their mature height is about 130 feet. The ponderosa, which gets its name from the ponderous appearance of its heavy wood, has bark that becomes deeply grooved with age, dividing into massive plates up to five feet long and 20 inches wide.

Ponderosas share the Transition Zone forest with smaller numbers of other tall conifers, including the giant sequoia that can live for thousands of years and reach a height of over 300 feet. The combination of summer warmth and perpetual moisture supports an array of wild flowers, shown opposite and on the next two pages. Meadows are filled with shooting stars, their petals bent back as if in motion. Heavily scented mountain misery carpets the open spaces. The Miwok Indians used an infusion made from mountain misery's pungent leaves as a cure-all.

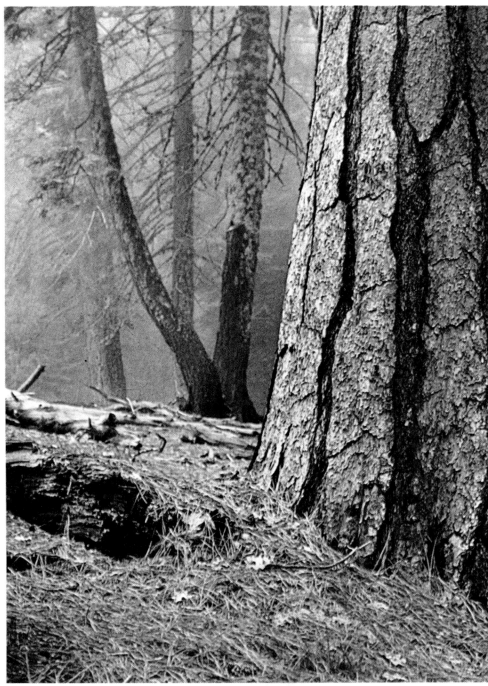

PONDEROSA PINE; WHITE FIR (LEFT BACKGROUND)

SHOOTING STAR

LUPINE

COW PARSNIP

MOUNTAIN MISERY

MUSTANG CLOVER

LARKSPUR

CRANESBILL GERANIUM

MARIPOSA LILY

HELIANTHELLA

The Canadian Zone: A Snowy Realm

Higher up on the mountains lies the Canadian Zone, marked by the tall, slender evergreens of its "snow forest." In this zone, which extends up to 10,000 feet on southern slopes, the winters are long and cold, extending from October to May and piling a blanket of snow 20 or 30 feet thick over the region. The brief summers are dry and cool.

A prominent tree in the snow forest is the red fir, a slender, beautifully symmetrical member of the pine family. The red fir grows to a height of 120 feet, with a trunk up to four feet thick. Its crown is rounded and its branches droop slightly, then turn upward in graceful arcs. Growing from their tips are long, purplish-brown cones.

Although the red fir is the natural master of the Canadian Zone, the lodgepole pine predominates on the fringes. The lodgepole is a smaller, more slender tree, 80 feet tall, with a trunk that is often no more than one foot in diameter.

The flowers shown on the opposite page bloom in turns after the snow has melted. The first is the bright red snow plant. Since this plant does not have green leaves it cannot use sunlight to manufacture food by photosynthesis, as do most plants; instead it feeds on decayed organic matter through its root system. In July the corn lily appears, and during August and September tiger lilies spring to life near the mountain streams.

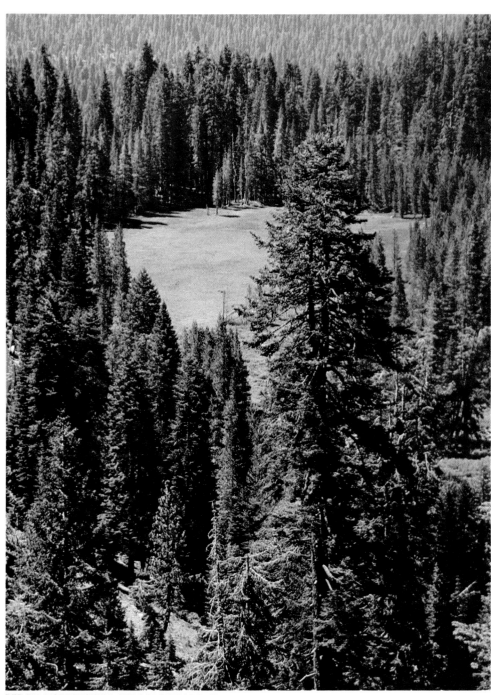

RED FIR (FOREGROUND) AND LODGEPOLE PINE

YELLOW MONKEY FLOWER

CORN LILY

CAMAS

SAXIFRAGE

SNOW PLANT

TIGER LILY

The Hudsonian Zone: Region of Struggle

There is a sense of devastation at the upper altitudes of the Sierra where the ground turns to rock and the plants are smaller and fewer. This is the true beginning of the High Sierra, the edge of another world—the Hudsonian Zone (or Subalpine Belt), extending from the boundaries of the snow forest to the timber line, beyond which trees cannot cope with the climate. Here the summer is brief, and even then the nights are so chilly that some specimens of the hardy plants that have adapted to sharp temperature changes succumb to killing frosts. Only the most rugged survive to perpetuate their species after the long, brutal winter.

The moist, rocky soils of this area support red heather, which grows soon after the heavy snows melt. In June and July the Indian paintbrush, which feeds in part on the roots of other plants, sprouts thin, tubular flowers. On rocky ridges, mats of yellow Sierra stonecrop and its purplish cousin, the Western roseroot, help to soften the ground.

The whitebark pine, though stunted, braves the upper limits of the Hudsonian Zone. Year after year drying winds and severe cold kill any branches that protrude above the deep snow; thus the tree can grow no taller than its protective winter cover. At the timber line, where the relentless wind leaves little snow in place, the whitebark grows prostrate, looking less like a tree than a twisted, tangled shrub.

RED HEATHER

SIERRA STONECROP

WESTERN ROSEROOT

INDIAN PAINTBRUSH

WHITEBARK PINE

The Arctic-Alpine Zone: The Edge of Subsistence

Whoever climbs to the summits of the Sierra will know why prophets have always sought mountaintops to commune with their gods. A strong, clear light falls on a frozen tableau: massive rock on massive rock with scattered lakelets to interrupt the vast cold emptiness.

The few species of fast-growing dwarf plants that live in the Arctic-Alpine Zone (or Alpine Belt) have had to adapt to cruel conditions. A permanent wind blows, sometimes more than 120 miles an hour. Temperature varies widely (even on a summer evening, it may fall to 28°). It seldom rains and most of the snow is blown away by the wind. What scant water there is seeps quickly into cracks in the rocks. Intense solar radiation poses the constant threat of dehydration.

Yet the plants survive. They avoid the wind by hugging the ground and hiding behind rocks. They preserve heat with foliage so thick and closely packed that the interiors of leaf clusters are sometimes 20° warmer than the air. Against dehydration they have adopted many of the structures of desert plants. Deep, wide rootstalks store food and water. Small leathery leaf surfaces have hairs that preserve moisture. Between the chinks in all this armor come the surprisingly delicate flowers shown at right. Clad in gentle colors, looking almost frivolous in this stark landscape, they are a tribute to the tenacity of life.

ROCKFRINGE

WALLFLOWER

PRICKLY PHLOX

YELLOW ALPINE COLUMBINE AND SIERRAN ROCK

4/ Four Sierra Creatures

Coyotes...are beautiful animals, and, although cursed by man, are beloved of God. Their sole fault is that they are fond of mutton. JOHN MUIR/ *AT SMOKEY JACK'S SHEEP CAMP*

The animal life of the High Sierra is quite sparse compared to that in more hospitable wildernesses such as the subtropical Everglades or in the lush rain forest of the Olympic Peninsula. Here in the Sierra, the wild things are, as the Sequoia ranger said, "right on the margin of existence, hanging on." Like that ranger, I cannot help but marvel at them, and the ways in which they adapt and survive. Among the denizens of the high country are four creatures that I find particularly intriguing.

THE PREDATOR/I first heard the voice of the coyote on a night in the northern Sierra when a harvest moon had just risen to touch the ridges above Alta Morris Lake in the heart of Desolation Wilderness. The night was cold, with gusts from the sundown wind buffeting the tents where the others were already sleeping after a long day in the saddle. I had stayed up, close to the pine-knot fire, to watch the moon. The wild creatures, too, were out with the moon, the predators ranging in the extra light; and some time after midnight, from the passes and along the meadows and draws, the coyotes began to call. The first sound was a single cry, high and far off and inexpressibly wild. It was like that of a wolf, but more contralto, and broken at the end into a series of shrill-toned barkings as though the coyote had run after his own howl and bitten it into small pieces. A second coyote answered the call. Then another and another took up the cry until our campground was wholly circled within a distant ring of primeval sound that lasted through half a waking hour.

In my next incarnation, when I hear that sound I will take up my knife or my stone ax and go out to hunt with my wild brothers. For their calling stirred something deep and quick inside me. It made me think then as I have ever since of the coyotes as my brothers, just as the boy Mowgli in Kipling's *Jungle Book* knew the wolves to be his brothers when he sat with them in a ring in the moonlight as they uttered the jungle cry, "We be of one blood, thou and I." But as a city animal bred away from the wild ways, the best I could do for now was go to my sleeping bag and curl up much too safe and warm, listening to the quavering signals of the unseen coyotes on the chase and feeling distinctly left out. I saw my first coyote only a few days later, some distance south of Desolation on a wooded plateau above Yosemite Valley. Again it was early evening, the hour when the midday heat is spent and the coyotes find the prowling more congenial among the cooling rocks and meadows. As I moved along a road a grayish full-ruffed animal loped from the edge of a stand of white fir. Its feet were tiny, its legs slender, its gait rhythmic and long and light as that of any ballerina. In its mouth it carried a squirrel that it had just taken. It gave me a short, appraising glance in the manner of coyotes, to see if I was threatening, decided I was not and ran another 150 yards in the open without looking again, to disappear finally into the shadows of a manzanita thicket.

The sight of the coyote was almost as moving as the sound had been, and nothing like the image of the scroungy, skulking barnyard cutthroat that is the coyote of almost any tale ever told by a sheepherder or cattle rancher. Stockmen hate the coyote with the same fearful passion that early settlers and their European forebears turned on the wolf. The popular notion has always been that all coyotes are sheep killers, calf slayers and chicken thieves. A senior biologist in the Department of Agriculture once called it "the arch-predator of our times," deserving no mercy.

As a result, the coyote was considered fair game for hunters, trappers and poisoners throughout the West. In 1915 the federal government joined forces with a number of states in a devastating program to reduce the coyote population. Bounties were awarded for dead coyotes, traps were set and, in some areas, poisoned carrion was prepared for them. In 32 years, the program administrators could claim an "official" coyote kill of 1,884,897 animals. The fact that the slaughter made very little sense ecologically or economically has not deterred those who continue to insist that the coyote is the nation's most destructive predator. Even though bounty and poisoning programs have been eliminated by the federal government and by most states, an estimated 75,000 coyotes are still killed each year, about 10,000 of them in California. While as many as 15,000 coyotes survive in the Sierra—many of them in the national parks, where predators are protected as part of nature's ecological balance—other animals have not been as fortunate. The last grizzly bear in California was reported seen in 1924, the last wolf disappeared from the Sierra about the same time, and the most recent count put the Sierra mountain lion population at fewer than 1,000.

Now, in effect, the coyote is the only predator left in the Sierra and it has its hands full. For nature put predators on earth for good reasons. Without them the land is much the worse, and so are the people on it—not to mention the soft-eyed forest creatures. Coyotes do indeed pull down an occasional deer. But in so doing they keep the herds strong. A healthy, full-grown deer, with its speed and slashing hoofs, is a match for any coyote. Therefore the coyote takes old, weak or diseased deer or winnows out the fawns. As a result, the herds do not grow so large they overbrowse their winter range to the point of subsequent massive starvation.

Coyotes also kill millions of rabbits, hares, ground squirrels, gophers and other small rodents, furry small fry that make up half the average coyote's diet. In regions where people have killed off predators like the rodent-eating coyotes, their erstwhile victims have nibbled the valleys and meadows bare and pocked the ground with so many tunnels and den holes that any horse or cow still interested in the denuded pasture is in real danger of breaking a leg.

Another fourth of the coyote's food is carrion, which someone ought to be cleaning up. And the remainder is a copious but economically inconsequential gallimaufry of grasshoppers and other large insects, mesquite beans, cherries, tadpoles, frogs, stranded fish, snakes (which a coyote will tease like a mongoose before killing), watermelon, juniper and manzanita berries, crayfish, apples, plastic surveyor's tape, duck eggs, garbage, old shoes and bits of leather harness, ducks (which the coyote sometimes catches by diving into the water and grabbing the duck from below), wild rose hips and almost anything else it can chew or swallow.

The Indians and early Mexicans, being in harmony with the land and its wild animals, knew all this and had feelings of great warmth toward the coyote. The *vaqueros* called it *amigo,* and learned to sing back and forth with the coyote at night. They claimed they could understand

A Sierra coyote finds its food supply reduced by early winter snows. Cold weather drives much small game into hibernation, but the omnivorous coyotes can make a meal of practically anything from berries to a discarded boot. A very adaptable animal, the coyote can survive the Sierra's brutal winters better than most of the region's wildlife.

coyote talk: high-pitched yips meant good weather; deep tones fore-told snow. Some Indians even worshiped the animal. Apaches believed they would become coyotes in the afterlife, a transfiguration I, for one, would be delighted to share. To the Miwoks the coyote was a god who modeled man in clay, breathed life into him at dawn and cried out in joy—as it still does at that time of day.

My own feelings toward the coyote are, as you may have gathered, somewhere between the Indians' spiritualistic worship and an ordinary wilderness traveler's plain admiration. I admire the male coyote as an attentive family man (although like even a human husband he may occa-sionally stray) who sometimes brings food to his pregnant mate, plays with the pups when the mother lets him near them—which is not often —teaches them to hunt as they get older, helps to move them to a new den if he senses a mountain lion or a hunter and affectionately touches noses with fellow coyotes after returning from a long hunt.

I admire, too, the coyote's marvelous speed and endurance. One coyote was clocked at close to 50 miles per hour in a short burst, others have been known to hold 30 to 35 for a full five miles; and in a season when the pickings are lean a coyote may range for 125 miles in a single hunt. Its ingenuity is simply awesome. It seems to know exactly where in a shallow tunnel a pocket gopher or a deer mouse will be. Going after a hare, which can run faster on a flat, the coyote sometimes hunts with a partner that lies in ambush until the hare is chased past a prearranged point. If the prey is a succulent but wary bird such as a goose, several coyotes may dance and cavort at a harmless distance to distract the fascinated bird while a confederate creeps up from the other direction. At bumblebee nests the coyote will wave its tail until all the curious or irritated bees have swarmed out, then stick in its nose and eat the honey. A coyote will follow deer-, duck- and quail-shooters, knowing it will get its share of cripples. In the snow time a coyote will stand near a bull elk as it paws through the snow for grass, aware that the hoofs will also turn up field mice. And a coyote will even adopt a road-grading crew so it can stand down-field from the bulldozer and wait as the machine scrapes up earth—and everything that lives therein.

Its courage is fierce and tends to be selfless. It will present itself as a lure to distract humans or animals from chasing its pups, and it will try to help a wounded coyote escape from hunters. Caught in a steel trap, it has been known to drag the device for weeks, somehow managing to find enough food to survive. And if it had not been able to eventually shake loose from the trap jaws, the coyote would probably have gnawed off a paw to get loose.

As for the killing of domestic animals, I find it hard to censure the coyote for pulling down an occasional calf. For one thing, the presence of even the most sluggardly and inattentive mother cow is likely to keep a coyote at a respectful distance. For another, stockmen tend to attribute all their losses to predators, even when there are no coyotes within 100 miles, and the real culprits may be poachers, or dogs that have succumbed to their ancestral predatory instincts. And finally, coyotes seem to prefer more traditional prey: a naturalist once saw a shaky little calf walk up and sniff at a coyote who was hunting field mice. The hungry coyote simply growled as might any busy adult at an intrusive child, and that was the end of the encounter.

It is quite true that some coyotes like mutton, and even better, lamb. But this kind of predation seems confined to a few individuals, just as burglary is the modus vivendi of only certain kinds of humans. In sheep country during a recent lambing season, when the pickings were most lush, the stomachs of only 15 per cent of trapped or shot coyotes showed sheep remains—and some of these remains were certainly carrion. The solution to the problem of the few sheep killers is to identify and trap them, as has been done in many cases, and leave the others alone, since they usually pass up lamb if a rabbit or squirrel is readily catchable.

Happily, both the state of California and the major federal agencies are coming to a much more benevolent, enlightened attitude toward the coyote. "Our own Department went out of the predator control business some time ago," says one California Fish and Game man. The U.S. National Park Service has had no predator control program since 1916, and the Forest Service people rarely go after coyotes, and are becoming less and less happy when others do so. Some ranchers and hunters still shoot coyotes on sight; and private trappers continue to take coyotes, for which there is a ready fur market. But these coyote killers are getting little official encouragement. In fact, some agencies have become downright protective toward coyotes, since every historical lesson shows that when predators are taken out, deer and rodents multiply rapidly and become major environmental problems.

"I think," says one ranger, "we're getting farther and farther away from the concept of good animals, like the deer and squirrels and such, and bad animals—the predators. I don't think it's our job to define good and bad that way. As we and the public get more educated about these things, we're learning to enjoy *all* wildlife. Besides," he added, in a moment of great illumination, "how can we say good or bad anyway, unless we do it in terms of man?"

His question challenges the historic attitude toward predators. And the fact that a responsible official was ready to ask the question suggests that at long, staggering last, 20th Century white man is beginning to move away from his ancient concept of a self-centered ecology. If he keeps moving, he may one day become as wise as the Indians. But he will never be so wise as my brother, the coyote.

THE BIRD/It would be awful to be called something as silly as an ouzel (pronounced *oo-z'l*), unless you were an oblivious, good-natured sort of clown who did not seem aware of what people were saying about you. Clearly this is the life style of the water ouzel, a slate-gray bird that, like a tiny deadpan comic, proceeds with stoic energy and unruffled mien to do everything wrong—and thrive. It is by some distance my favorite of all Sierra birds because, with the exception of hawks and eagles, whose power and purpose I admire, I tend to regard most birds as basically rather silly. The water ouzel, being the silliest, is therefore a favorite.

First of all, it does not seem wholly aware of the fact that it is a bird, although it is a member of the thrush family. It seems mixed up about what birds do: fly in the air, build nests in quiet places, pull worms from the earth. The water ouzel builds its nest in the wettest and noisiest place imaginable, behind a waterfall or right next to the edge of a cascade. Though each nest is a brilliant piece of architecture, it does not look like a nest at all, but more like a beehive or a Watusi hut. Dome-shaped with a single arched doorway, it is made of pieces of green moss so fresh and so tightly woven that they continue to grow even after the nest is finished. From this soggy but elegant headquarters the ouzel sallies forth to look for food, which it does almost exclusively at the bottoms of pools and running streams.

At first glance the ouzel seems wholly unequipped for such underwater work, having neither webbed feet for swimming nor the shovel bill that helps many water birds dredge up their dinner. The ouzel usually feeds in the shallows, sitting on a stone and bobbing its head into the water every three or four seconds to turn over pebbles and rocks in search of the insect larvae that cling beneath. If that does not work, it flutters to midstream and dives to the bottom, where it walks upright on clawed feet for a minute or more, calmly poking around just as though it were plucking seeds from a lawn. During such submarine forays, the ouzel closes a scaly trap door over each nostril to keep water from com-

A bird that can walk underwater, a water ouzel prepares for one of its curious stream-bottom strolls in search of food. Ouzel fancier John Muir described the bird as "a singularly joyous and lovable little fellow as smoothly plump and compact as a pebble that has been whirled in a pothole."

ing in. At the same time it protects its eyes by lowering over them a filmy membrane that, like a skin-diver's mask, keeps the water from interfering with its vision.

If the current is flowing fast, as it usually is in the Sierra, the bird walks upstream so that its beak and head deflect the current and its whole body is often encased in a clear bubble of subsurface air. And whenever the rushing stream becomes too powerful for the ouzel to keep its feet, it simply spreads its wings and begins to propel itself in a manner analogous to flying underwater, perfectly sure that this is a sensible activity.

Unlike most other birds, the water ouzel is not concerned with variations in the weather, no matter how violent. Its relatives in Alaska and Asia dive into cascades when the thermometer is at 50 below. In the Sierra at 11,000 feet in a mid-January blizzard, with four feet of snow already on the ground and the open streams a mass of snow sludge and ice shards, the ouzel, bobbing about looking for frozen bugs, will be as unconcerned as if it were the height of summer.

Occasionally the ouzel gets around to behaving like ordinary birds, but not very much like them and not very often. As birds will do, it preens itself by plucking oil with its bill from a gland at the base of its tail and lubricating its feathers. But the ouzel does so on a heroic scale, being something of an aquatic superbird; it has an oil gland 10 times larger than that of land birds the same size that it uses to waterproof its feathers. Sometimes the ouzel actually flies in the air. But whenever it does so it tries to stay directly over a stream, following every bend, rising and dipping over rapids in a course parallel to the contours of the water. At a waterfall it will go into an abrupt power dive to the bottom of the falls, where it levels off just over the water.

Perhaps the most startling thing of all about this bizarre and homely little creature is its song. It is perfectly lovely, a pure sequence of melodic trills with a tone somewhere between a flute and a clarinet. As it does everything else, the ouzel sings where and when it chooses, even in the teeth of a Sierra gale. And it does so with a style and assurance indicating that it is totally certain—even if nobody else is—that any ouzel is not only a proper bird in its own right, but very likely the best of all possible birds.

THE FISH/I never regretted killing fish until I caught a golden trout. Before that I had the common attitude toward fish as fair game to anyone with hunger pangs or an impulse for (continued on page 114)

Collecting food for winter, a pika carries grass to dry in its rockslide shelter.

A marmot pauses between quick mouthfuls to scan the horizon for enemies.

Mottled fur camouflages a California ground squirrel.

The Small Mammals' Dangerous World

In the Sierra—and elsewhere—the little creatures shown here lead all the orders of mammals in both numbers and diversity. Most are rodents, whose ranks include hibernators (marmots), nonhibernators (porcupines), tree dwellers (flying squirrels), burrow diggers (mountain beavers), nut eaters (chipmunks) and plant eaters (pocket gophers), insect and meat eaters (grasshopper mice), and species that eat almost anything.

Different as the species are, most share the rodent trait of curved, prominent front teeth that grow continuously. This distinguishes them from rodent-like mammals such as the pika, a rabbit relative with four front teeth. True rodents have only two. Tireless gnawing or chewing keeps these teeth filed down to sharp cutting edges. The filing is vital: if a beaver is unable to gnaw small trees and branches, its incisors grow until they lock its jaws.

Rodents and many other small mammals are fecund enough to offset their high mortality rate. Relatively defenseless, they serve by the thousands as staples or snacks for local predators, furred, feathered or scaly. If predators did not prey on them, mammals such as the prolific voles—two-ounce mouselike creatures bearing many litters of three to seven young each year—could overpopulate and strip their habitats.

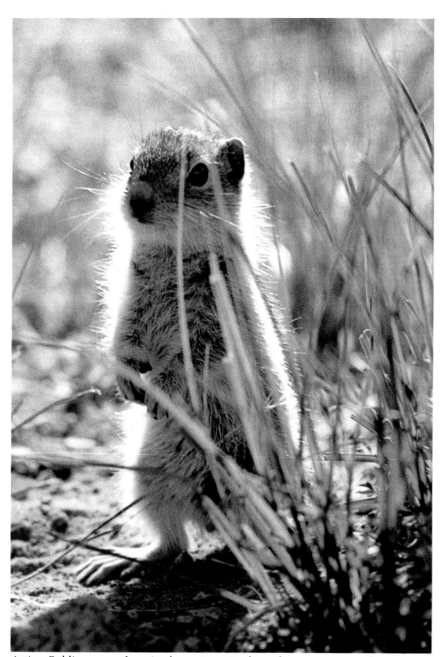

A tiny Belding ground squirrel squats on its haunches to peer over low grasses.

low-risk sport. My first encounter with a golden came on one of those superb frost-cold Sierra mornings along Rock Creek near the headwaters of the Kern River. The sun was too bright and, by the time I was fully organized, already too high for good fishing. But we had time to spare. A planned trail ride was delayed by the nocturnal departure of two of our mules and one horse, whose tracks indicated they had wandered toward their home corral. The packer grumpily started after them at dawn, muttering through mouthfuls of canned peaches about the ancestry, morals and I.Q. of all livestock. I decided to use the hour or two of his travail by taking a walk alongside the creek with my rod and a handful of splendid little flies tied to order by a Connecticut neighbor's son after he had done much research into the particular entomology of this very corner of the mountains.

The walk in itself was delightful. At each bend and riffle the creek subtly changed the low, chuckling tone of its voice. I moved downstream to a place where a waterfall had carved a perfect pool—deep water with a rock in the middle where a trout could lie still, out of the current, then flicker off to strike at whatever food might float into sight.

I fished the pool carefully, staying in the shade as much as possible, squatting down on my heels to cast so as not to throw a disturbing shadow into any fish's line of sight. After perhaps an hour I managed to drop a caddis fly right at the bottom of the falls, so that it swirled in a natural manner just past the rock and perhaps six inches under the water. A shadow darted out and I felt a delicate, almost subliminal touch on the line. By happy chance I was raising the rod tip for another cast, so the hook set.

In perhaps three minutes I had the fish ashore. It was 10½ inches long, its back and tail a glistening olive green, the body shading from yellow to rich gold along the sides to vermilion down the center of the belly. The gill covers gleamed bright red, as did the lower fins, with an added touch of white along the edges. The tailfin, dorsal and entire back were speckled with black dots, while oval patches of gray punctuated the golden side strips. The trout was as striking in color as many tropical fish, far too handsome to be yanked out of the water for someone's breakfast; and I immediately wished that the creature were back swimming free beneath the falls. Unfortunately, the hook had set deeply in the mouth cartilage, which I tore in trying to disengage the fly; there was no purpose in returning the crippled fish to the water. I took it back to the campground and showed it to the ranger with whom I was riding.

He told me the golden was a separate species of trout (*Salmo aguabonita*), native only to the Kern Plateau in the southern Sierra Nevada. The species had evolved sometime after the Pleistocene when volcanic upheavals changed water flow to isolate a number of rainbow or cutthroat trout (there is debate about which species was involved) in the creeks of the granitic tableland south of Mount Whitney. There, either by coincidence or by the natural adjustment of protective coloration, the fish slowly took on the hues of the yellow volcanic sediments and reddish granitic sand in the stream-bed gravel.

Thus, old-school Sierra watchers claim the golden is a Kern River rainbow once removed. Superficially it seems to be, since the golden hybridizes freely with the rainbow to produce fertile young, and its native waters once flowed gently into the Kern before the volcanic activity along the stream beds created cascades the fish could not negotiate.

The first goldens ever to journey outside the Kern Plateau made the trip in a coffeepot carried in 1876 by a lumberman who dumped them into the Cottonwood Creek drainage where he hoped they would provide him with good sport as he worked his nearby sawmill. They did, and their progeny have since supplied superb fishing through much of the Sierra and wherever else they have been planted, for the Cottonwood Lakes, under the loving eye of the California Department of Fish and Game, have become a golden trout breeding ground. Each year the department takes upward of 700,000 eggs to incubate and then sow as baby fish in some 150 lakes and streams.

The goldens, whether Kern Plateau natives or transplants, are the fussiest, subtlest feeders of any fish I have encountered. And while this characteristic provides just the sort of masochistic pleasure a fly fisher dotes on, it makes the golden a poor competitor for food against such other immigrant species as the brown and the eastern brookie with which he may find himself sharing a pool. For this reason, as well as the golden's deplorable habit of breeding with the rainbow to produce less desirable hybrids, the department has become more and more selective about where it drops its goldens, and chary of allowing other species to invade established golden trout habitats. The department has tried to maintain some waters in the High Sierra as pure golden territory, temporarily poisoning them to clear out other species, and then restocking them with golden fingerlings. The department has provided further protection for the golden trout, but from humans this time, by forbidding all angling in four of the 13 Cottonwood Lakes and by lowering daily catch limits in the remaining lakes and feeder *(continued on page 118)*

Basking in a Sierra stream, a golden trout enjoys cold, well-aerated waters at elevations of 8,000 feet or more. A native of the southerly region of the Kern Plateau, the golden was unknown in the northern lakes and streams it now populates until anglers started to stock those waters in the 1870s.

A mountain lion patrols its well-defined territory, hunting for game and repelling invaders throughout an area of up to 125 square miles.

A Last Stronghold for the Big Cats

The mountain lion in action is a model of graceful ferocity; in an age when predators were hated, Theodore Roosevelt called it "the lord of stealthy murder." The big cats (often called cougars) weigh as much as 225 pounds. They creep up silently on their prey, then explode in a short, swift charge. They are powerful enough to kill a 200-pound mule deer with one bite and drag the carcass uphill for miles to a rocky lair.

The lion's much maligned role as a predator explains why it is rarely seen in the Sierra today. In 1907 California's mule deer, which supply about 75 per cent of the cougar's diet, were dangerously depleted by human hunters; in a misguided effort to help the herds regain normal size, the Division of Fish and Game offered a bounty on mountain lions. In 56 years, $388,730 was paid out for the killing of 12,461 of them. As a result, the state's lion population now stands at an estimated 2,400, with 800 spread out through the vast reaches of the Sierra.

Yet according to one study, a mature lion eats only one deer a week. The Sierra mountain lion probably never had much effect on the local deer population, and state officials belatedly recognized this fact by repealing the bounty in 1963. A moratorium on hunting the big cats helped to increase their numbers to the point where the population is now controlled by natural limitations rather than by traps and rifles.

A snow-spattered cougar pauses in the hunt.

streams; the limit has dropped from the standard 10 to a more modest five. In the late 1960s Inyo National Forest ecologists initiated a proposal, subsequently approved by Congress, to reclassify and rename part of the Kern region as the Golden Trout Wilderness. One of the planners, an ichthyologist and a key figure in the maintenance of the Sierra as a sport fishery, suggests the day may come when the golden trout receives the same no-kill immunity that all national parks animals now enjoy.

"When I was a kid," he says, "there was a willow bush by this one stream where I could catch all the fish I wanted in an hour. Now my kids are happy if they catch one or two. And I can see this philosophy extended to the point where people may think of the golden as something to catch and admire and put back, rather than eat."

I applaud this reasoning, both as a sporting proposition and as a matter of gastronomics. I prefer the taste of brook trout, whose flesh generally strikes me as being firmer and moister. I suspect, however, that there are those who will disagree with this judgment. And I am certain there will be shouts of rage at any throwback rule imposed in the High Sierra, where at least 75 per cent of back-country visitors carry flyrods or spinning gear. But this majority of anglers may have an even greater shock ahead.

"Eventually," adds the ichthyologist in a burst of purism that even a part-time bumbler like me finds a bit extreme, "we may not catch the goldens at all but just look at them and appreciate them as a living part of the wilderness."

THE MONARCH MANQUÉ/In the world of people it is seldom that the most attractive man is both a posturing male chauvinist and a gauche lover. But among the animals of the Sierra, this is most certainly the case. In all the high country there is no creature more striking, more regal than the California bighorn, or mountain sheep. A fully developed ram may stand 35 inches at the shoulder and weigh up to 250 pounds; his magnificently curved horns, nearly five inches thick at the base, sweep through arcs that may be a yard around and bring the total weight of the animal's head to as much as 30 pounds. Unlike the mule deer, which sheds its antlers each year, the mountain sheep carries its horns all its life. They first appear as buttons on its head when it is a lamb of three months. They keep growing up and back and then down, where they stop developing in ewes but continue to grow forward in rams until at the 12th or 14th year the horns enclose a full circle if the tips are not broken off in fights or accidents. A ram thus adorned carries his head very erect, as though inordinately proud of his magnificent crown. But the fact is, the horns weigh so much he has to hold his head erect to keep his balance.

Like so much else about the bighorn, their running is a thing of pure beauty, especially when they are moving among the ledges and crags of the apparently suicidal terrain that is their natural habitat. They travel in summer at altitudes of 10,000 to 14,494 feet (the summit height of Mount Whitney), along the eastern crest of the Sierra, plunging at a full gallop through country where a hiker or even an experienced mountaineer would creep with a rope and a prayer. The bighorn can scramble down a 150-foot cliff in a matter of seconds, half jumping and half tumbling from one tiny ledge to another six, eight or 10 feet below with no hesitant reconnoitering. And it can go back up again almost as fast, grabbing onto the rock with broad, flexible hoofs equipped with a special rubbery pad.

Moving across loose rock on an avalanche slope, the sheep relies on a superb sense of timing. A naturalist once saw a band of 14 bighorn, including three rams led by an older ewe, running along a headwall at the top of a canyon toward a 60-degree chute filled with the unstable jumble of loose rocks called talus. As the leader approached the chute on solid rock she put on a burst of speed that let her almost float across the talus with lightning-quick scrambling strides until she bounded onto solid footing on the other side. The sheep crossed one at a time and in a line so that none would be hit by rocks dislodged by another from above. After each animal crossed, it turned to wait until the entire band was safely across the chute.

Such sightings of the bighorn are rare. For along with the mountain lion and the wolverine, the mountain sheep is about the hardest of all Sierra animals for a wilderness traveler to see. This is in part because the historical reaction to the bighorn has been to shoot it, close to the point of wiping out the species. Bighorn meat is very good indeed. One mine cook reported killing 50 bighorn all by himself in the winter of 1895—a dozen years, incidentally, after a moratorium was called on bighorn shooting in California to prevent the extermination of the already hard-pressed species. Today there are fewer than 30,000 bighorn sheep of all species in the contiguous United States, as compared to an estimated two million in 1800. And of this remnant, only 250 bighorn survive in the Sierra, scattered in small bands between Mount Langley in the south and the Mount Baxter-Sawmill Pass area in the north.

Besides being few in number and fond of impossible terrain, the bighorn are also hard to spot because of their coloration and deliberate

A band of bighorn sheep from the Mount Baxter herd pauses during the annual descent to its wintering range in Inyo National Forest.

caution. Their hair and horns are a dun color, the precise shade of the rocky country they inhabit. When grazing they move in studied slow motion, instinctively aware that quick movement catches the eye of any prowler. Between snacks they lie curled up and still in a shallow depression pawed from the earth, looking for all the world like just another boulder. I have never seen a bighorn in the Sierra, although I have seen their tracks in the granitic sand of a broad alpine barren some 12 miles northwest of Mount Whitney. I have no doubt, however, that they have seen me. Few creatures on earth have better eyesight than the mountain sheep. Another naturalist, studying a band of sheep so far away he had to use eight-power field glasses, noted that whenever he made the slightest movement every sheep in the band—made up mainly of ewes and lambs—would instantly raise its head to look even though the observer's clothes blended in color with the rock against which he was standing. If she is sure she has been seen and lacks an escape route, a ewe will sometimes place her body between the observer—who represents peril—and her lamb.

It would rarely occur to a ram to do such a thing. In fact, rams are rotten fathers. As noted earlier, they are the worst kind of male chauvinists, with a powerful sense of themselves and a penchant for traveling in privacy-seeking bachelor bands. They seldom, if ever, spend time with the lambs they have sired or with the ewes that bore their progeny—except when it is time to change location seasonally or to mate. Alas, when his great moment of mating arrives, the lordly bighorn ram becomes a posturing, bumbling high-country buffoon.

The mating, or rutting, season in the Sierra starts in late October, whenever the first ewe happens to come into heat. As that occurs the rams lose all interest in bachelor living and start chasing ewes with great enthusiasm but not necessarily much success. When a feeding ram catches the scent of a ewe in heat his head snaps up and he stretches his neck forward with the nose straight out and his head tipping steadily from side to side. Usually two or more rams pick up the smell simultaneously. Then they set out after the ewe at a fast trot. They bowl over any animal between them and their intended, stumble boorishly on stones, sometimes on their knees but never stopping.

If the object of all this confusion is an older ewe, she may stand around and wait for the rams to arrive. A younger ewe will often take off at top speed.

Meanwhile the rams, whose amorous impulses seem not only gauche but frequently short-lived, may turn away from the ewe to square off in a ritualistic and almost totally harmless joust to determine the all-important domination order. For openers there is a good deal of groaning and snorting and milling about between two rams. This can last for a couple of hours, and were it to occur between combatants at a modern prize fight or an ancient tournament at arms, the crowd would be bored silly. But to the intent rams it is all part of the mandatory facedown.

From time to time during these preliminaries the rams will approach each other and, standing head to rump, each tries with his forefoot to hit the other in the genitals. Whether or not either party is scored upon, there is no evasive action taken nor any indication of pain or irritation. When the kicking is over, a brief period of camaraderie follows, with much licking of each other's sides—whereupon the erstwhile combatants amble off to feed. However, they keep a close eye on each other, signaling ceremonial ferocity by pawing the ground and giving off a few more snorts. Suddenly, as though upon a silent signal, both will rear, their front legs flailing the air. Then they drop onto all fours, apparently to get fully set. Finally they rear once more, draw a bead on each other down their noses and charge at top speed with heads lowered to crash together with a BONK that is audible for three quarters of a mile. The collision, occurring at speeds from 50 to 70 mph, generates an impact that has been estimated at 2,400 pounds; from which the immediate effect upon the rams is usually zero, though a lifetime of such jousting can chip or break off the tips of their horns.

They just stand there a moment, then back off and go at it again. This sometimes continues on and off all afternoon, with about five-minute intervals between charges until the two rivals have had as many as 40 brain-rattling collisions. At no time during a charge does either one so much as think of chickening out. On the contrary, they aim and time their rushes to create dead-on collisions, and if one ram leans a little to the side, the other leans to compensate. Meanwhile the ewe has long since wandered away from all this manly assertion to feed by herself or has run off with a frisky young ram ignored and unchallenged by the combatants. In the special world of the bighorn, it would not matter if she stayed around. For the rams, especially in the preliminary stages of the rut, seem much more interested in dueling than in love-making. The jousts establish the superiority of one over the other. When that becomes clear the rams just stop banging heads. If the ewe is still around, the winner may claim her or amble off to seek another mate. Either way

the preliminaries of actual courtship and sometimes the attempt itself
are so brief that it is small wonder the ewes are so uninterested.

The species has managed to weather an eon of such posturing grace-
lessness at the mating game. But it has barely managed to survive the
onslaught of humans into its habitat. Even though the legal shooting of
sheep ended almost a hundred years ago and poaching in the Sierra is
now negligible, there are simply too many people trampling through the
bighorn's terrain. All the California bighorn live within the Inyo National Forest and the eastern fringe of Sequoia National Park, where total
recreational visitors increased from a quarter of a million in 1950 to well
over 20 million in 1980. The presence of all these people has made the
bighorn skittish and recessive, pushed onto ranges where survival is
more difficult than in their normal, more congenial habitat. During the
1950s and 1960s the California bighorn sheep population declined by
almost 45 per cent as the animals retreated into the most barren and
remote corners to get away.

Fortunately the federal and state officials have noted the threat of
human intrusion and have begun to do something about it. There is a
firm commitment to build no new foot or horse trails into bighorn country, and to let the existing trails erode away. Overnight camping in bighorn country is now prohibited, and permits are required to enter certain very limited areas over designated trails only. Thus the decline in
sheep population was reversed in the early 1970s, assisted by the program of trapping healthy young sheep from the remnant bands and re-
leasing them into some of their old habitats. In recent years the bighorn
have increased by 15 per cent, and the continued survival of this imper-
iled species seems assured.

NATURE WALK / Along McGee Creek

PHOTOGRAPHS BY DAVID CAVAGNARO

Every mountain stream, like a living creature, has a character all its own. As the stream flows away from the source—a glacier, a lake or a spring—it takes its shape and its voice from the land through which it travels. The stream in turn gives to the land the priceless treasure of water, which means life to the growing things along its banks.

In time, the stream on its journey may swell to such power that it recarves the very face of the mountains where it was born. Or it may appear as fine and delicate as a necklace, all the while eroding away ever so gently the ground over which it courses until it finds an ending in a pond or a bog or a larger river. Yet with the ending the stream's existence is not over, for it is continually reborn at its source.

Thus each stream endures as an individual phenomenon and as a lasting fascination to the wilderness traveler who walks carefully alongside it, moving quietly and dwelling at leisure on the variety of plants, birds and other creatures that exist so compatibly along the course of the stream. McGee Creek, in the northernmost section of Kings Canyon National Park high in the central Sierra, provided this special fascina-

tion for me on one July day's walk.

The upper portion of McGee Canyon, a glaciated basin that gives the creek its source and direction, is typical rockbound Sierra terrain, much of it more than 10,000 feet above sea level. The creek itself links the 10 connected ponds of the so-called McGee Lakes with Evolution Creek, a broad flow that picks up the waters of McGee Creek and moves them downstream to the South Fork of the San Joaquín River.

My companion and I first encountered McGee Creek after riding our horses to a glade not far off the John Muir Trail, roughly at the stream's mid-point, where the altitude is about 10,400 feet. Some three miles farther up the canyon and 600 feet higher lay the lakes, which were to be our goal for the day.

It was not long after 10 o'clock in the morning when we first arrived at the creek. The horse trail reached the bank at a bend where the water flows easily through a small meadow and a copse of lodgepole pine.

At brookside we dismounted, tied up our stirrups and reins, and waved our horses on to loose-herd with the packtrain headed for our campground higher up while we made our acquaintance with the stream.

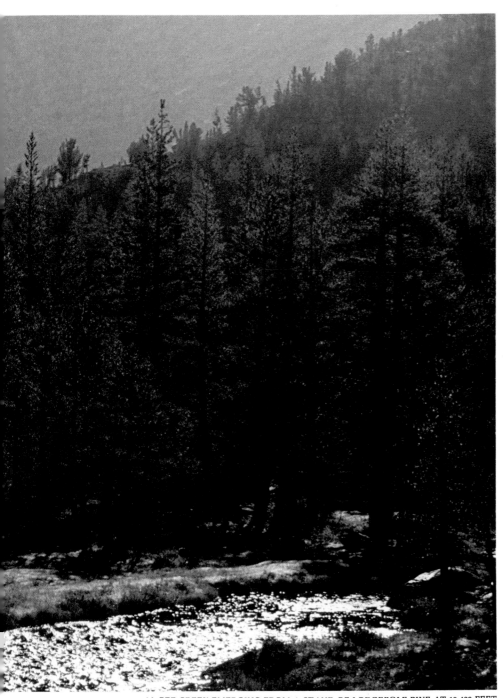

McGEE CREEK EMERGING FROM A STAND OF LODGEPOLE PINE AT 10,400 FEET

I was struck at once by the water's richness: here and there beneath the surface the larger rocks were vibrant with coverlets of clean green algae. The splash zone at stream's edge and the small boggy tables just above held thriving colonies of mosses. Among them, the decorative spires of swamp whitehead poked thigh-high from the sodden ground, their tops bent and arched in random directions. At the tip of each branchlet hung six to a dozen spiny white pompon bursts.

Of all the mosses assembled here, the most intriguing was *Polytrichum,* which in a crucial step of the reproductive cycle sends out hair-thin

SWAMP WHITEHEAD

stems capped by pods that may contain dozens of spores. These spores are the key to a remarkably complex process that has several stages.

Upon maturing, the spores are scattered by the wind—and the movement of water in the stream —and finally settle in the moist soil and molds near the stream's edge. In time, the spores develop into new green moss plants, each one having both male and female sex organs, known as gametophytes. When mature, and if the moss has picked up at least a thin coating of water from the stream or dew, the male and female parts then enter the final step. The male sperm begin to swim through the moist film covering the moss, while the egg-bearing organs emit a sugar that spreads through the adjacent water. The sperm are drawn to the sugar, more powerfully as the concentration increases, until they arrive at the eggs, which then become fertile. The result, in a process that repeats itself until the coming of winter, is a new generation of spore-bearing capsules on the tops of long red stalks.

Mixed in with the moss were stems of wild onion, their roots in

MORNING SUN ON A SMALL RAPID

the boggy ground they prefer, and long strands of sedge. Close by stood the three- to four-foot stalks of corn lilies with their drooping, elongated leaves, and a cluster of delicate Jeffrey shooting stars. Beneath one purple-rimmed blossom a tiny mayfly, with translucent wings folded, was hiding from the wind that was buffeting the catkins of streamside

willow and shaking golden streamers of pollen from the overhanging lodgepoles. A sluggish Behr's sulphur butterfly slowly awakened at its perch among the grasses.

Morning—a Mighty Mushroom

Nearby, the base of a lodgepole pine supported an explosion of a mushroom that scientists call *Lentinus lepideus,* known more colorfully as train-wrecker fungus. Reaching sizes up to three feet square, it grows throughout much of the continent on dead conifers or oaks, and is notorious for attacking railroad ties—especially those not treated with creosote—and eventually rotting them to create the threat from which they get their name.

In a patch of ooze water just below the mushroom, the gray, narrow-

THE REPRODUCTIVE SPORE PODS OF POLYTRICHUM MOSS

WAKING: A BEHR'S SULPHUR BUTTERFLY

ly tubular larval cases of caddis flies littered the pine duff on the bottom. The caddis flies had deposited their eggs here last summer, and over the winter the eggs hatched into larvae, then into pupae, building these tubular cases as a protection from birds of prey and perhaps as camouflage (they closely resemble tiny sticks).

Late Morning—Haven for a Snake

Within a radius of another three or four paces were half a dozen other species of insects—all food for a garter snake we saw slithering about in the meadow grass a few hundred yards farther upstream. It is surprising, in fact very rare, to see snakes of any kind at these altitudes. They have little time to find a living here, since they fall into a torpor with the first frost in September and then must hibernate through the many months until the weather becomes endurable late the following spring. Also, at timber line and above, there are too few places where a snake can hide from the quick, deadly Cooper hawks, which like nothing better than reptile. In fact, the high country is so hostile and the odds for a snake are so poor that I often wonder why any of them bother to try to live this far up in these mountains.

The answer in this particular case is probably McGee Creek's congenial surroundings. Being on the western side of the Sierra crest, the creek basin receives much more moisture, in the form of both snow and rain, than the parched stream courses on the east slope, which sometimes dry out completely during the summer. High

A TRAIN-WRECKER FUNGUS

ridges to the east, west and south of the stream give some protection from the wind, and yet the valley is wide enough through its middle reaches so that the stream banks get sunshine from 9 or 10 in the morning through late afternoon.

The central portion of McGee Creek itself would be ideal for snakes at almost any altitude. Here the channel widens and occasionally braids into easy meanders. Dozens of small yellow-legged frogs inhabit the margins of these branchlets. And here, as elsewhere throughout its entire length, McGee Creek is alive with immature golden trout, small enough to be snatched from the water by the swift strike of an alert snake. The creek is embraced by a broad meadow full of grass and

A COMMON GARTER SNAKE

small bogs in which fat insect larvae hatch by the millions. Polliwogs dart about in the backwaters. A garter snake with any degree of enterprise can do a lot better than survive on this rich diet. And if a hawk should skim by, the snake can either hide in the deep meadow grass or, in a real emergency, dive under the stream's waters and stay submerged until the trouble passes.

Noon—a Pine Cone's History

Thus the snake survived, but examples of the inevitability of death and decay (and their relationship to the living) were everywhere. It was a little after noon when we came upon a thoroughly chewed whitebark pine cone, long ago fallen to the ground. It was dotted with penicillium fungus (the same growth that

A BEE FLY SEEKING ITS HOST

is cultivated to make the drug), two kinds of slime mold and a cup fungus. Some time back a mountain creature, probably a raucous, aggressive bird called the Clark nutcracker, had robbed the cone of its nuts. We saw a nutcracker perched on a rock near a whitebark pine; it usually knocks the cones off the tree, and later, using its bill like a combination of pick and crowbar, pries out the sweet green nuts.

At almost every step along the banks was more testimony to the wealth of summer life by the stream, and of the close connection between water and plants and insects and animals. Each pool held flickering shadows of golden trout, lazily feeding or darting away from our sudden presence, sometimes in such haste

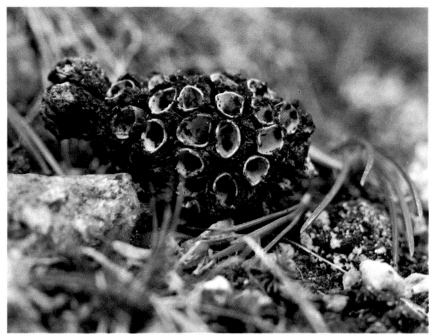

THE CONE OF A WHITEBARK PINE, ITS NUTS EATEN

THE CONSUMER: A CLARK NUTCRACKER

and so close to the surface of the water that their tail and dorsal fins left tiny rumplings of wake.

The feeding fish often worked in circular patterns, drifting out into the stream and down-current; then, just before being sucked into a rapid they would swim up into the still water again, each fish in search of the bountiful food available in the short summer months: aquatic larvae of the caddis flies, for example.

In these high altitudes, where permanent running water is rare, each species of streamside plant plays a role in the life of some creature. In the midafternoon heat, a bee fly was hovering near a delicate, daisylike erigeron. But it might only have been pausing in its search for another flower that is closely connected with its life cycle—and for the bee from which it gets its name. The Newberry penstemon, or mountain pride, has a wide mouth that gives easy entrance to any roving bee—or bee fly. In gathering pollen, the bee may attract the attention of the bee fly, a predator that sneaks up on its prey in a manner that circumvents the bee's barbed defenses. It does not attack directly; what it is likely to do is follow the bee and lay its eggs near the hive. The larvae from the fly then proceed to eat young bees as well as stored honey and pollen. The larvae invade the closed-off cells of the bee's nest, where they eventually become adult insects whose only purpose is to find another bee's nest and begin the process once more.

Before we encountered the bee fly a thunderhead had been building be-

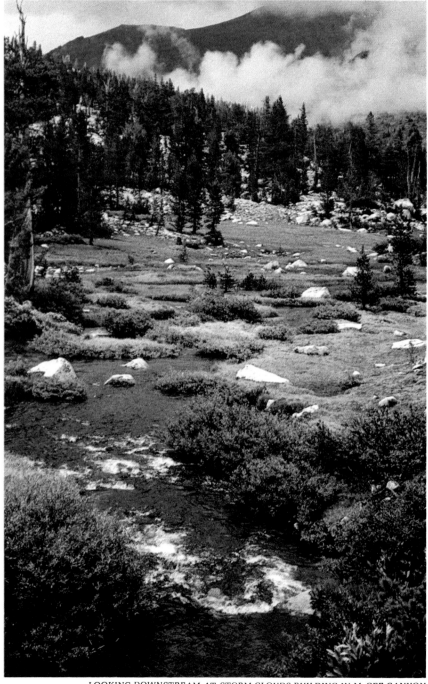

LOOKING DOWNSTREAM AT STORM CLOUDS BUILDING IN McGEE CANYON

A CREEKSIDE PATTERN: RAINDROPS AND SEDGE

A MOSQUITO EMERGING FROM ITS PUPAL SKIN

A YELLOW-LEGGED FROG AWAITING A MEAL

AFTER THE STORM: SUNLIGHT ON GLACIAL POLISH NEAR LOWER McGEE LAKE

hind the heights ahead of us. Now rain came in on the westerly wind with stormy rumblings close behind. The rain, running across the rocks of the creek basin, gleamed against the sheen of glacial polish on the surface of the granitic bedrock.

The rain started with a rush. But after a few minutes, it settled to a fine, steady downpour that promised to last some time. We decided to wait out the storm under the inadequate cover of a stand of lodgepoles near the creek. I am certain that the plants and creatures, even the stream itself, were grateful for the rain. The mountain frogs, their legs flashing as they plopped in and out of the stream, seemed to leap with more verve than before the storm. However, I was not thankful. Every half-stagnant pool on the course of McGee Creek, from the summit to the stream's junction with Evolution Creek, harbors its mosquito larvae and pupae, called tumblers. And as the rain eased, the mosquitoes seemed to emerge from the tumblers in greater abundance, adding to my annoyance at being wet.

The earliest mosquitoes to emerge in the spring, called snow-pool mosquitoes, hatch out of meltwater as soon as the sun can raise the water and air temperature even one degree above freezing. The rest take their turn, hatching throughout the summer. As we watched, one of the current crop, a tiny comma-shaped pupa, floated to the surface of a puddle, then split open its skin and flew off as a mature insect as soon as the wind dried its wings

and hardened its external skeleton.

At that point my curiosity about mosquitoes evaporated. They rose in such clouds that a bare neck or forehead became the instant feeding ground for a half dozen or more insects. I found little comfort in the fact that the female mosquito bites me only because she needs the protein from mammalian blood to nourish herself so that she can carry eggs. Much more agreeable to contemplate was an insect I saw making holes in something besides me. A

A SAWFLY ABOUT TO DEPOSIT HER EGGS

sawfly—a kind of wasp—had lit on a nearby penstemon, where, using the sawlike appendage in its rear end, it was busy puncturing the underside of a leaf and laying its own eggs in the cuts.

As the afternoon deepened, we approached the stream's upper reaches. Above the main meadow the creek basin narrowed into a little rocky valley with a rich, hanging bog on one side, established where water, seeping from rock, has allowed moss to grow and build up a moist cover of soil. This bog was filled with red and yellow columbine, the multiple blossoms of elephant heads, gooseberry currant and glorious red splashes of paintbrush.

Late Afternoon—Dwarf Plants

In this upper altitude, as we climbed along the last cascade toward the source lakes, the plants and insects were changing noticeably. The taller stream-bank willows were giving way to the tiny dwarf species, whose three- to four-inch height contains all the makings of a true tree with root system, trunk, branches, leaves and catkins.

Dwarf blueberry also appeared, and the lupines, whose stems farther downstream had been a foot long or more, now stood no more than six inches or so high. Back from the stream, the cold- and wind-resistant buckwheats crouched in tight bunches. And along the stem of one plant crawled a wingless crane fly, one of the several high-altitude insect species that through evolution have lost their wings; the mountain winds have too often made flight futile.

When we reached the summit lakes a setting sun had smeared a spectrum of pink and red and orange across the departing remnants of rain clouds. A few mountain sparrows still hopped about looking for insects and worms, and an alpine chipmunk held its paws in an attitude of incongruous prayer as it munched its last meal before sundown. Soon bats would be out to gorge on the bonanza of mosquitoes.

A WINGLESS CRANE FLY

HUMMINGBIRD'S FAVORITE: PAINTBRUSH

A CLOSER LOOK: PAINTBRUSH AT DUSK

NEARING McGEE'S SOURCE

AN ALPINE CHIPMUNK EATING THE DAY'S LAST MEAL

We were now in the granitic bowl beneath the ragged metamorphic masses of Mount Huxley and Mount McGee, where the creek has its beginnings in a chain of 10 lakes that lie at altitudes between 10,800 and 11,000 feet. The sides of the bowl are spotted with mattings of whitebark pine, smeared with lichen where moisture slides thinly over the rock and laced by cataracts of meltwater from crescents of lingering snow. Scoops of gray-black pebbles tumble down the summit wall of Mount McGee. These come from glacial moraines, half a dozen of them left behind by a melting glacier, some now holding lakelets of their own and each a reminder of the force of ice that carved the McGee Basin.

Dusk—at the Source

The lakes themselves are the clearest water, a pale glass green, melted out of the snowpack. As can be seen from the air, or on a map, they are arranged in a rough circle like a chaplet; the three largest ones are connected by inlet streams to a string of smaller ponds, lying upslope to the southwest, that are the ultimate source of the creek. The lakes are not rich in chemical nutrients; however, the movement of water within the lakes is so slow that the minute plant algae and insect larvae in them have a tendency to take hold and grow, thus multiplying and contributing their own fecundity to the developing food chain that will eventually support larger insects and fish downstream.

Since the lakes are shallow the sun can warm them during the brief summer, stimulating organic growth and giving off relatively warm water to McGee Creek as it emerges as a cataract tumbling from the last lake.

As the time approached to make camp for the night, we came upon one final act in the round of life that turns near these mountain waters. It was the blossom of a shooting star, crimson pink with purple edges. As dusk fell, a pair of ants were

A SHOOTING STAR AT LAKESIDE

starting up its lower stem, evidently to capture the aphids that were nestled down within the blossom, their hip glands full of sweet nectar. By morning, we guessed, the ants would have carried the aphids down into an underground pen, to be kept and tended for their nectar. In the morning, we looked; ants and aphids were gone. The flower remained.

THE SOURCE: LOWER McGEE LAKE

5/ The Cabinet of Curiosities

*...At last they looked from their prison
over drifted walls of dazzling white, that towered twenty feet
above their heads.* BRET HARTE/ THE OUTCASTS OF POKER FLAT

The month is April. Spring is in the valleys below the Sierra, and along the eastern scarp the snow is melting up the mountainsides in a ragged line of rotting drifts. In the timbered canyons the ground is bare to 7,000 feet, and on the rock faces of the scarp above the Owens Valley the snow line has backed up all the way to the crest, leaving only tendrils of white reaching down the flanks wherever there is a gully's shade or a northerly exposure. But beyond that crest in the high world of the Sierra heartland, winter's cold hand has not relaxed its grip, and much of the land retains an arctic look. West of Mount Whitney, where three of us have been living above 10,000 feet for the better part of a week, the meadows lie beneath sweeps of snow, frozen hard in the morning though melted by the midday sun into sharp, close-set corrugations. North for more than 180 miles the few roads across the mountains are closed as they have been since November, blocked by drifts. Within the great bowls where the mountains' contours trap the damp winds sweeping up from the Pacific, the snowpack remains 12 to 20 feet deep in places. Scattered glades of young hemlock on the forested western slope have been bowed and bent so deeply by the weight of snow that the trees lie supine, entirely covered beneath the drifts, where they will remain until the final melt releases them and, with a soft rush, they spring erect once more.

The high country seems to be clinging to a final moment of rest under the diminishing white blanket. And the quiet pervading the wilderness suggests that only in winter is the Sierra truly wild and natural, as it once was. "The thing that saves this country is the winter," a fisherman had said last fall. "For nine months a year it lies under snow and has an opportunity to rejuvenate itself, to restore itself. If the wilderness got the kind of use for 12 months that it gets for a couple of months in summer, there'd be nothing left."

At the moment we seem to be the only intruders upon an enormous stretch of alpine landscape, and we have a serene feeling that plenty is left of the wilderness, especially that most precious commodity—solitude. True, some 200 miles north thousands of skiers are crowding the slopes on the wilderness fringe at resorts like Squaw Valley, Sugar Bowl, Alpine Meadows and Heavenly Valley, and closer by at Mammoth Mountain in the central Sierra. Yosemite, too, has its own modest ski area; and spotted along the snowed-over track of the Tioga Pass road perhaps half a dozen winter campers are roughing it with nylon tents and goose-down sleeping bags. But that is all. We came into the high country, two Sequoia National Park rangers and I, by helicopter some days ago, skimming over an 11,000-foot pass near Mount Whitney, to be dropped on the snow of Crabtree Meadow three miles southwest of the peak. Since then we have spent our days traveling overland on skis with our food and clothes and sleeping bags stuffed into 40-pound packs. Nights we have bedded down in back-country cabins maintained by the Park Service in cooperation with the California Department of Water Resources' snow-survey crews. The surveyors come here at monthly intervals in winter to gauge the water content of the snowpack, and to predict the amount of water likely to run off in the spring and eventually to accumulate in lowland reservoirs. This snow-survey work is critical to the well-being of California. Los Angeles and San Francisco get much of their drinking water from the runoff of Sierra snow, and farmers in the Central Valley look to the Sierra reservoirs and west-slope rivers for economic survival.

When we first flew in, though reveling in the absence of man, we felt a little deprived because of the apparent scarcity of wild creatures in the winter wilderness. Thoreau once said, "In winter, nature is a cabinet of curiosities, full of dried specimens, in their natural order and position." And indeed the snow on the Sierra meadows and passes, seen from a low-skimming helicopter, appeared bare of wildlife tracks—no coyote, deer or, in fact, any overt sign that animals were abroad or that the plants had begun to stir with the imminent onset of spring. The deer left these elevations when the November blizzards pushed them down to their winter foraging grounds in the foothills and valleys. They went out quickly with the first storms, moving down the bare, wind-blown ridges and avoiding gullies where accumulating drifts might trap them into the agony of starvation—or a swifter death from the coyotes that follow the herd to pick off faltering strays.

Now in April the deer are luxuriating among the shrubs and green grasses of the newly warmed lowlands, and it is a bit lonely up here without them. For in this part of the wilderness, a national park in which all animals are protected from shooting, the deer during the summer season are both abundant and bold. From July through September hardly a day passes without half a dozen of them drifting past a given campground or standing to watch the passage of a packtrain, their large eyes soft and unafraid like those of the animals in Edward Hicks's painting *Peaceable Kingdom*. They will be back soon, moving into the high mountains as tender shoots sprout from the snowbrush behind the line of melting drifts. But for now, the kingdom is empty of them.

It is empty, too, of the summer scramble of golden-mantled ground squirrels and chipmunks. The ground squirrels are all sleeping below the earth in tunnels or in burrows lined with shredded bark. As they lie curled into fat doughnuts of fur, their bodily commitment to hiber-nation during its deepest period is so complete that, to judge by vital signs, they are barely alive. Their breathing has slowed down from a norm of about 200 respirations per minute to four, their heartbeats from 200-400 to perhaps five. Their body temperatures have sunk to near freezing, and for about six months they have had no interest what-ever in the waking world. The chipmunks are somewhat more active, oc-casionally foraging abroad and then returning underground to drowse near piles of stored seeds upon which they nibble during their inter-mittent awakenings.

With no rodents yet at large, the predator birds—the golden eagles, red-tails and the smaller Cooper hawks—that cruise the timbered meadows from spring through fall are still downslope where the pickings at meal-times are better just now. Even the fish seem to be keeping themselves scarce. The high lakes have remained frozen; and beneath the ice the trout, their metabolic rates slowed by cold, are nosing about lazily to feed on the plankton and midges that have survived the 32° to 39° sub-marine temperatures. Most of the streams, however, have broken loose from their overarching snow tunnels to move as dark meanderings among banks of sugary masses of decomposing snow crystals. At the edge of Crabtree Meadow where the helicopter dropped us, Whitney Creek is live and full and clear, apparently as congenial a fish habitat as it ever is in summer. Yet whenever we visit the creek to fill our water buckets we note no golden trout either feeding or holding in the pools. Nor are there any fresh depressions in the stream-bottom gravel to indicate that the lengthening days and more intense sunlight of spring have yet triggered the breeding instinct and impelled the goldens to start digging out new spawning beds with their fins.

In fact the only vestige of wildlife visible when first we came into the wilderness was a sparse fluttering of the small birds that are willing to make do on the spartan diet offered by the winter Sierra. Some chickadees and a homely but hardy little creature called the rosy finch were busy pecking on the chilled pine nuts and dead refrigerated insects that melt or blow out of snowbanks.

It seems surprising that these tiny birds, even though protected by layers of feathers, should be able to survive year round in the High Sierra. But the past days in the high country have brought us several other more fundamental surprises. Among them has been a realization that the high-country winter, though justly famed for the violence of its climactic storms, is often quite docile and unthreatening, and sometimes not much colder than the summer.

From the very first day of our trip the weather has been consistently mild, almost idyllic. Afternoon temperatures have been about 50°, too warm on these cloudless days for sweaters or even for the gloves that prevent blisters from the rubbing and chafing of the ski-pole straps. By evening the thermometer has dropped near freezing, but the air is so dry and still that we find ourselves comfortable in T-shirts whenever we go outside to fetch water, split wood or wax our skis. Even at the grim hour of 4:30 a.m., when we roll out to get moving before the night-frozen snow turns too mushy for easy ski travel, the temperature has never been colder than 22° above zero. Such balminess in the high mountains is an unaccustomed joy for all three of us. I am an Easterner who has frozen his face and fingers more than once in the biting cold of a Vermont ski slope, and my two companions are natives of Colorado and Montana where cattle can die frozen in a standing position during a blizzard at 50° below.

It is true that on this Sierra trip we have been lucky to hit the warm days of a dry, early spring. Nevertheless, entries in the logs kept in each snow-survey cabin confirm that gentle weather is not uncommon in the high country: "clear and warm," "clear and sunny today," "six-eight inches new snow, very little wind," "sunny in the morning." An account by an early snow surveyor named Orland Bartholomew of an odyssey he made in the winter of 1928-1929, beginning on Christmas near Mount Whitney and ending April 3 in Yosemite Park, has such comments as these: "No temperature below zero was recorded above 11,000 feet during the entire winter. . . . Many streams were found flowing almost unobstructed by ice or snow, even above 10,500 feet. The minimum temperature [January 10] on the summit of Mount Whitney at midevening was 26 degrees F." Even John Charles Frémont, that redoubtable chronicler of toil and hardship, revealed in his journals that the winter weather during his 1844 crossing of the Sierra was not always bad: "The purity and deep-blue color of the sky," he wrote, "are singularly beautiful; the days are sunny and bright, and even warm in the noon hours."

As with the weather, so with snow depths. They turned out to be nothing like the extremes I had expected. On this point, however, the old journals as well as some of the more modern accounts are superficially misleading, for they dwell on the most awesome of the Sierra winters. A diary of 1850 signed "Alice" tells of a three-week blizzard that left drifts 50 feet deep. In the winter of 1867 a village at Meadow Lake in the northern Sierra was buried so completely that the only way people could move from house to house was through snow tunnels dug across the main street. Eighty-five years later at Yuba Gap the crack stream-lined train *City of San Francisco* stalled in snowdrifts and marooned 200 passengers for 96 hours before an escape path could be cut through to them. And in the winter of 1969 a world-record 11 feet of snow came down on Big Whitney Meadow in one 48-hour period in February. Even the conservative snow-survey logs for that year record heavy falls all over the high country: "Feb. 14 . . . Cabin was completely buried under 14-16 feet of snow. It took over an hour and a half of digging in a snowstorm to enter. Stovepipe was clogged. . . ."

It is true that at various times these sudden extremes of weather have made the Sierra a lethal place for anyone who allowed himself to be caught in the wrong place at the wrong time. The ill-advised and poorly equipped Donner party of 1846-1847 tried to start across the mountains too late in the season and foundered, tragically, in the drifts of an abnormally early and heavy snow year. In 1867 avalanches killed 20 men working on the Sierra link of the transcontinental railroad; and

A stand of stately white firs bears the weight of a heavy springtime snowfall in the middle elevations of Sequoia National Park.

in the 1970s more than a dozen skiers and climbers were swept away or died of exposure when they dared the wrong mountain at the wrong time. Perhaps the worst hazard of all is the wind, which can blow at cruel velocities. Summit-country gales have screamed at a recorded 120 miles per hour and more, whipping the snow with such ferocity that in one cabin a room was one quarter filled overnight by snow forced through the only aperture—a keyhole.

Such winds can kill a human or even a wild creature, not only by sheer force but by producing a weather equivalent of cold called windchill factor, which can pull winter temperatures down to arctic levels. On a day when the thermometer reads 20°, a 25-mile-per-hour wind will create a weather equivalent—i.e., windchill factor—of 15° below zero; and on a rare zero day with 35-mile-per-hour winds the windchill factor will be minus 52°. This windchill, together with the long season of subfreezing nights and the sporadic occurrence of severe snows, accounts in large measure not only for the arctic appearance of the high country but also for the arctic adaptation of so many of its plants and animals.

Thus, the threat of deep winter pervades and controls all life. Yet now in April, normally the time of greatest snow accumulation before the major spring runoff, the placid look of the High Sierra indicates that massive snow depths—like low temperatures—are really the exception. The meteorological record confirms this impression, both as to frequency and locale. The Sierra enclaves such as Mammoth Mountain and the Donner Summit area, which regularly report depths of 25 feet, are at comparative low points in the crestline, where the Pacific air can slide through and dump its snow load. But above the 9,000-foot line, as in the region we are traveling west of Whitney, precipitation drops off and the average snow depth on April 1 for the southern Sierra is a modest 5 to 6 feet. And two winters out of three the snowpack is below average. This dry, warm year the snow measures only about two feet, with many of the south-facing slopes baked completely bare and the wind-blown summits as barren brown now as in October.

Another surprising fact about the Sierra winter is the abundance of wildlife that shares it. The high country, although far emptier than in the summer months, is not really so dead as first impressions suggest. In fact the wild country has offered us excerpts from some fascinating stories as we have skied and climbed cross-country, keeping a close eye on the surface of the snow, on the trees and on the streams. Heading off from the Crabtree ranger cabin we saw the tracks,

Under the soft mist of early-morning fog, a melting blanket of snow frames Wolverton Creek in Sequoia National Park. The quickening freshet of meltwater signals that the mountain spring is just around the corner.

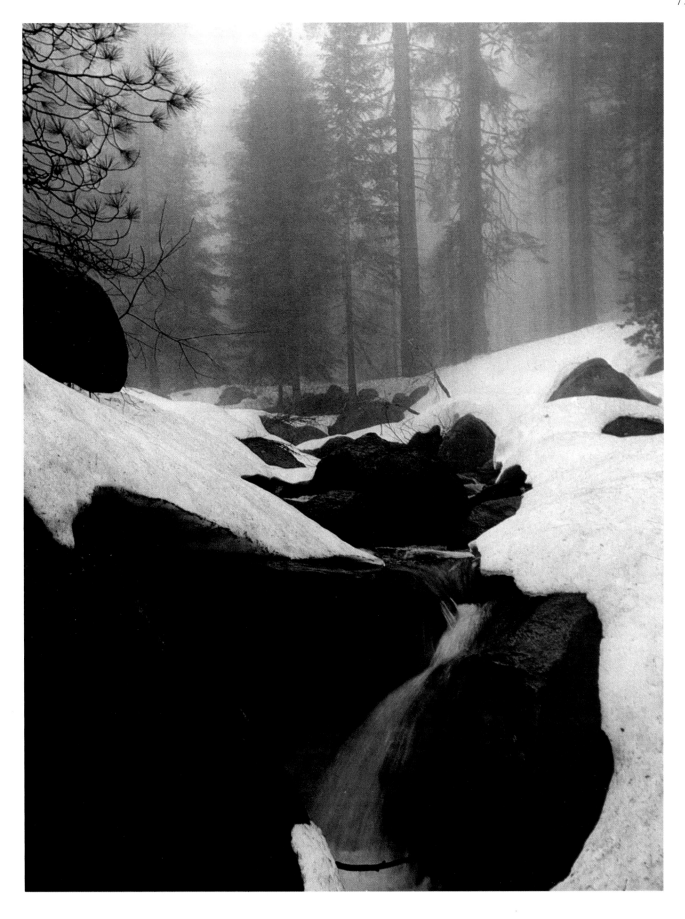

frozen in the snow and perhaps a week old, of a white-tailed jack rabbit that had run up the south bank of a stream in a pattern of light measured bounds. This lanky high-altitude creature, whose fluid gait is nothing like the comic bobbing of a garden rabbit, is able to stay alive and healthy at this season in the high country by nibbling on tree bark or dried grasses. Few four-footed animals venture higher or have made an easier adjustment to austere surroundings. During his 1929 journey, Bartholomew saw several of them sitting about on the bare windy summit of 14,042-foot Mount Langley.

Near the jack rabbit tracks on a patch of open ground we found a series of little meandering dirt piles that looked something like the tunnel roofings left on a lawn by moles. These were made by pocket gophers, chunky brown burrowers with long foreclaws and buckteeth for excavating. When the snow covers the ground, the pocket gophers tunnel into the drifts just above earth level. These snow tunnels are used as storage spaces for the dirt that the gopher continues to excavate from his deep earth tunnels all during the winter. He packs the loose dirt from his digs as tightly as possible into the snow tunnels, making a series of dirt corings in the snow. When the spring snowmelt starts, the corings sink to the ground surface and lie there in the twisting, elongated mounds that caught our eye.

A few yards beyond these corings was the first set of fresh tracks we had come upon. A mountain coyote had come down a draw at a dead run —probably within the past two days. His tracks appeared again and again as we climbed. There were no other tracks of any kind on the line of his run, indicating that he was not on a hunt when he went by. Privately I hoped he would be drawn tonight by the cooking smells from our cabin, because I love the sound of his cry and I wanted very much to hear him call to us from high on some nearby ridge.

In a high valley not far from Whitney Creek, at a steep place between two trees spaced about four yards apart, we came upon pairs of paw marks the size of a child's hand denting the snow in spacings of perhaps a foot. The prints were old and melted down though the contours of the pads still showed dimly. Our first guess was wolverine, but that was probably wrong since the wolverine, a surly carnivore who demands enormous amounts of both food and solitude, is perhaps the Sierra's scarcest and surely its most unsociable creature. More likely it was a pine marten, an agile arboreal weasel who likes to travel and hunt through the trees. One of his favorite foods is the chickaree, or

Douglas squirrel, which sees no need to hibernate during the winter. And though we ourselves have seen no such squirrels, the marten's tracks in the forest indicate that there are some around.

It is also possible that the marten was prowling for Sierra grouse. If so it was gambling on a very elusive, albeit sumptuous, meal. The grouse is a heavily feathered bird whose cast-iron digestive tract lets it flourish through the winter on a diet of pine or fir needles. Being not only plump and juicy but also resident the year round in the high country, the grouse is much admired by predators. As a result it is at times a deeply cautious bird, about as easy to catch unawares as a Las Vegas blackjack dealer. If the marten manages to catch the grouse, however, the resulting banquet will solve all its nourishment problems for at least a week.

These are the kinds of stories that are written on the snow for anyone who takes time to read and interpret them. And it occurred to us as we studied the marten's tracks that they were perfect evidence of the relationship of all things in the wilderness to each other. Until it becomes the prey of a coyote or mountain lion, the pine marten sits atop a pyramid of life that begins far out on the Pacific Ocean—that began, in fact, far back in time when these mountains first formed. The mineral-rich soil of crumbled bedrock in the back country provides a seedbed for the pines. The pines sink roots into that soil and are nourished by meltwater from the snowpack, born of clouds that formed over the Pacific. Once grown the pines provide seeds for the chickaree or needles for the Sierra grouse. And they, in turn, are the food that sustains the pine marten. Knowing all this, John Muir wrote, "When we try to pick out anything by itself, we find it hitched to everything else in the universe." This is as true in winter as at any other time—and thus I find the winter wilderness not a cabinet full of dried specimens, but a rich and peaceable kingdom of creatures and growing things, each meeting the daily hardships of cold weather in its own way, or simply sleeping until, with spring, the living is easier.

Spring in the Sierra

Springtime comes late to the High Sierra. Advancing slowly from the foothills to the uplands, it seldom makes its appearance much before mid-May, and it is often delayed until early June by a severe winter. The first sure sign of its arrival is the sound of flowing water—trickling rivulets and splashing streams, created or swollen by melting snows. And then the still, cold mountains come quickly alive.

The thick snowpack is relatively fast to melt in the mountain meadows, where only brief morning fogs screen the warming sun. The spongy flatlands sop up the moisture and burst into bloom, their flowers unfurling in broad swatches of contrasting pigments: creamy corn lilies, lavender shooting stars, pink or red monkey flowers. Most pervasive of all Sierra blossoms, monkey flowers bloom in any wet place—seepages, bogs and stream banks—from the lowest to the highest elevations.

As the meadows dry out, mariposa lilies (page 152) unfold cup-shaped flowers of various colors, all of them irresistible to flies, butterflies and bees. The insects, including clouds of mosquitoes that have hatched in puddles and bogs, keep the Sierra birds busy from dawn until twilight,

when swarms of bats emerge to take up the chase.

The lower meadows may have been abloom for weeks before the snow begins to melt in the forests at the upper altitudes. Here the floral display is less extensive but even more varied. Of the Sierra's 1,400 kinds of flowering plants the greatest number dwell in these wooded areas; among them are such early-blossoming exotics as the crimson snow plant (page 149).

At altitudes above 10,000 feet, on the rocky windswept slopes leading to the Sierran summits, flowers rarely bloom before mid-July, and their whole growing season—spring, summer and fall—is crammed into just two months. Of the species native to the upper heights, perhaps the most evanescent is a small phloxlike mountaintop perennial called the sky pilot (after the slang term for chaplain—i.e., someone who shows the way to heaven). The sky pilot blooms only between late July and early August, and its blue flowers, growing in low clumps, hold their bloom for scarcely more than a few days. The wonder is not that they fade and shrivel so soon, but that they manage to blossom again at the next late spring thaw.

Imprisoned in ice at an altitude of 11,500 feet, a spiky seed stalk of timothy grass awaits the liberating warmth of the spring sun. For plants high up in the Sierra, the end of winter is retarded by nightly freezes continuing well into July.

A patch of snow (above), melting slowly on a mountainside, erodes into miniature peaks and valleys. After a snowy winter, the thick pack may not melt off completely until mid-August.

Hibernation over, ladybird beetles (right) emerge glistening wet from rotten logs and rock crevices to sun themselves. After a few days, they fly to the lowlands to feed on aphids.

A fast-growing snow plant, one of the first to appear in the forests, pokes its scaly head through a mat of twigs and pine needles. Within a week or so, the fleshy stalk grows to a height of eight to 12 inches. Then its scales curl back, exposing about two dozen bell-shaped crimson flowers. The plant is reputedly poisonous, but the Indians used it as a remedy for toothache.

Adaptable and persistent, a yellow-flowered cinquefoil flourishes in the meager soil of a rocky niche, watered into vigorous bloom by spray from melt-swollen waterfalls. In the middle altitudes, cinquefoil grows to four feet, but at higher altitudes it becomes a stunted, ground-hugging plant.

Far left: Springing up from the floor of a warming meadow, mariposa lilies put forth elegant blooms and arching, lineal leaves. Most of their blossoms are creamy white, though rarer species produce flowers of yellow, red, lilac and purple. The bulbs from which the lilies grow were an important food for several Indian tribes. The Miwoks roasted and ate them gratefully as a gift from the gods.

Left: The tender sprout of a thistle breaks the raw earth shortly after the snow melts. The smooth pale shoot scarcely resembles the bristly mottled plant that soon develops from it.

Top right: A young mayfly, drying out its membranous wings on a rush branch, has a short life span as an adult. Myriads of mayfly nymphs become aquatic insects in peaceful meadow pools, where most are gobbled up by rainbow trout. Those that survive to grow wings quickly breed a new generation, then sleep and die—within two days of the time when they emerge from the water.

Bottom right: A young newt lurks beneath a frond of cliff-brake fern, protecting its sensitive skin from the sun and concealing itself from prey and predator. The newts hatch from eggs in ponds and streams and spend their first winter under the ice as larvae. By spring they reach full growth (seven inches long) and develop legs and lungs for land travel. But they are seldom found very far from the water.

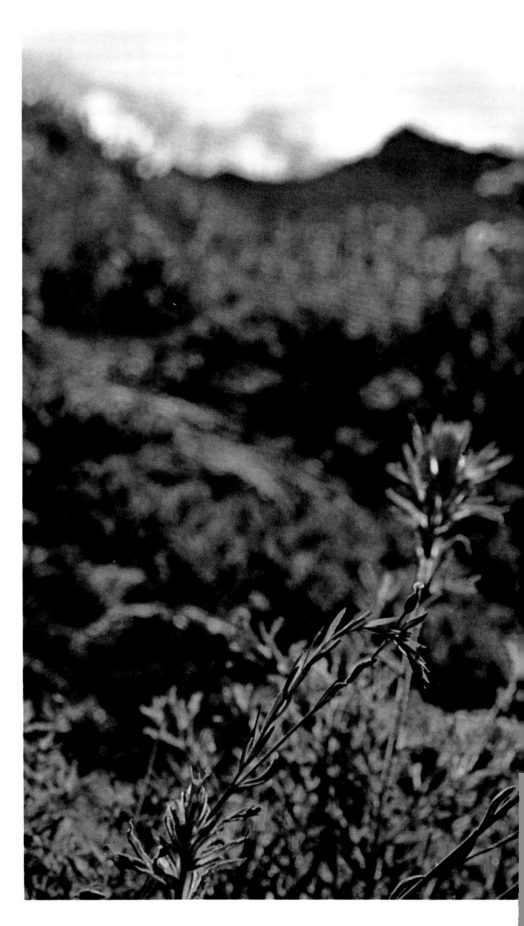

Blooming on an alpine slope 11,400 feet high near Elizabeth Pass in Sequoia National Park, paintbrush (left) and blue flax announce the coming of spring in mid-July. Both plants keep their blossoms through summer and fall, seasons crowded into seven or eight weeks; then they fade with the first hard frosts in the beginning of September.

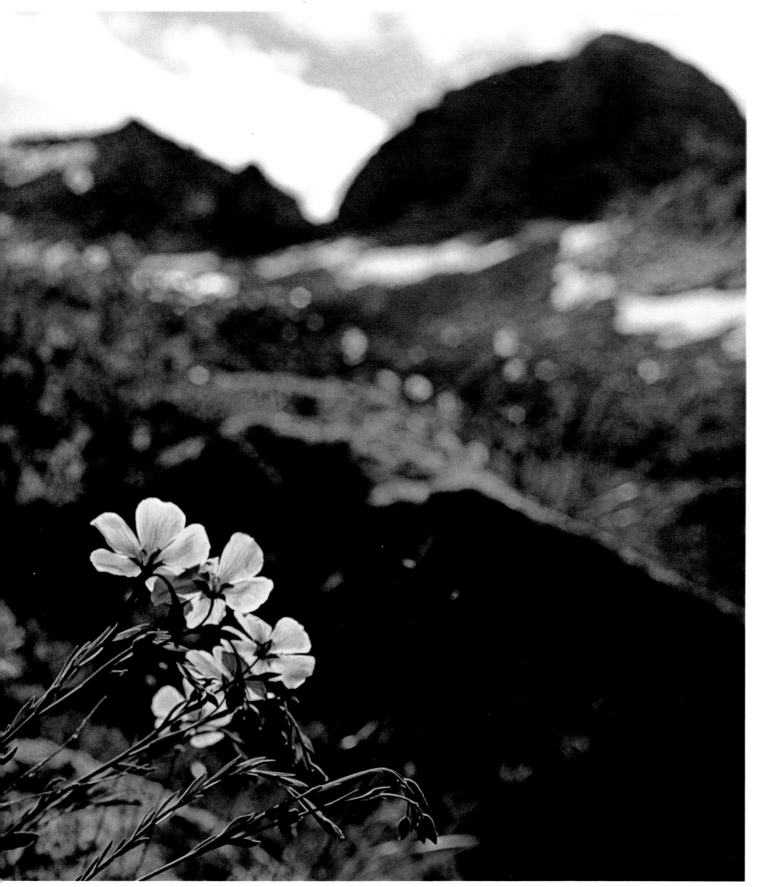

6/ Preserving What Is Left

The real significance of wilderness is a cultural matter. It is far more than hunting, fishing, hiking, camping, or canoeing; it has to do with the human spirit.

SIGURD F. OLSON/ *THE SPIRITUAL ASPECTS OF WILDERNESS*

More than a century after the first step to preserve the Sierra wilderness was taken with the establishment of Yosemite Valley as a state park, one of the keepers of today's vast domain of Sierra parks and forests looked out upon the work of saving the wild land for the people and liked what he saw. In one year, 10 million Americans had come bustling around the fringes of the back country. Three million of those had gone into the real wilderness to camp, to hike, to ride, to fish, to hunt, to cut timber, to work mining claims, to take pictures, to play guitars, to drink beer, to make love, to study rocks, to admire animals, to find peace, to find themselves and, in my own case, to write a book. Projections for the rest of the century indicate only slight increases in the imposing numbers of annual visitors, however, as state and federal caretakers increasingly resort to a system of licenses and permits to prevent overcrowding on the most popular trails and campsites.

In a way, the Sierra has become a victim not only of its established renown but of its ready accessibility at a time when the appetite of an urbanized nation for the wilderness experience is growing steadily. Many of the families that have moved to the sprawling residential communities of central California and western Nevada have been lured by the nearness of the Sierra. They make up many of the 40,000 visitors who descend on Yosemite Park every summer weekend, taxing the facilities to the limit.

The Park Service constantly seeks ways to make better use of crowded parks such as Yosemite—restricting cars to the periphery, encouraging guided group tours, requiring permits for overnight camping. At the same time it is caught in the ceaseless struggle between environmentalists, who want to expand and protect the remaining parcels of wild countryside, and the exploiters, who would tap the mineral resources and harvest the timber of the wilderness. For a while, the environmentalists had the upper hand. The Wilderness Act of 1964 not only guaranteed the sanctity of existing Wilderness preserves but established a protective umbrella for a projected 55 million additional acres. In the Sierra alone, the size of the officially designated Wilderness would almost double if 1.45 million acres of back-country national park land was included. Such an addition would be a distinct and welcome change from the historic trend of a wilderness whittled down by politically powerful industrial interests.

But the pendulum began to swing in the other direction as the 1970s got underway. As of 1981, there had been no substantial additions to the Sierra's wilderness acreage, and the exploiters were finding sympathetic ears both in Congress and in the federal government. Reduced funding was making it difficult to maintain existing park land and almost impossible to purchase additional land. But so far any serious threats to the Sierra have been effectively countered by law and by organized groups of wilderness lovers. For example:

☐ When the Forest Service sought competitive bids for development of a roadless Sierra enclave called Mineral King Valley into a year-round recreation area, Walt Disney Productions won with a plan to build a ski and summer resort that would cost up to $35 million and include a multilane access road through part of Sequoia National Park. The Sierra Club sued the government and carried the issue all the way to the Supreme Court in an attempt to kill the plan. The Sierra Club lost, but the project was suspended. In 1978, Congress transferred Mineral King Valley to national park status, adding it to the adjacent Sequoia and Kings Canyon National Parks.

☐ Though a handful of gold miners still scratched away at a few parts of the Sierra, empowered by a clause in the Wilderness Act permitting mineral development for 20 years, the filing of fresh claims had dwindled until the rapid rise in gold prices during the 1970s made such small operations profitable. There now appears to be little likelihood that mining will end when the permissive clause expires in 1984, but environmentalists hope to limit future operations.

□ Rangers long ago chased cattlemen and sheepherders from the parks, although grazing is permitted in a few patches of wilderness where the practice was established before the area came under the coverage of the Wilderness Act. In a couple of places the ban on such livestock extends beyond the boundaries defined by the Wilderness Act to adjacent areas of national forest where available forage has been set aside for deer and bighorn.

□ High-country lumbering has been forbidden in the parks and national Wilderness. In the less protected national forests, preservationist pressure has prodded Congress to hold hearings on the lumbering technique called clear-cutting, by which loggers remove most of the trees from a forest area, leaving it an unsightly scar of stumps, shrubs and bulldozer tracks until a new generation of trees has had time to mask it. "For the first time people are noticing the practices in forests near them," said a Congressional aide, "and they don't like what they see."

□ Even the highway builders, once encouraged by none other than John Muir to build access routes for Sierra campers, have been cut off at the pass. When a trans-Sierra highway that would bisect the John Muir Trail near Mammoth Mountain was proposed, no fewer than 10 preservationist organizations came down against it.

Thus the state of the Sierra wilderness has been effectively maintained and, in some areas, even enhanced. Much of the improvement has come from the efforts of the Forest Service to protect the wilderness areas within its jurisdiction. Although the national forests, unlike the national parks, have been available for private development, the Forest Service has become increasingly concerned about the preservation of the natural environment. "I think this new concern with the environment is heaven-sent," said one park superintendent. "It's the best thing that's ever happened to the wilderness—as long as it hasn't come too damned late." During my visit there was scattered evidence throughout the Sierra wilderness that the hour might indeed be growing late. Yet largely because of the heightened environmental awareness, for every new problem faced by the wilderness, its protectors seemed ready to apply remedies.

Symptoms of overuse were plainly visible. The main trail from Echo Lake leading to Desolation Wilderness, like so many other back-country arteries, had become wide and pounded. The trail starts between a folksy village store and a boat-launching ramp at the edge of a parking lot, then climbs through a series of steps made from creosoted railroad ties set athwart the path. At intervals trail signs say PUBLIC BOAT DOCK ¼ MILE or BOY SCOUT CAMP 300 YARDS. On Echo Lake a speedboat cuts the surface into outflowing chevrons while shuttling as a water taxi between the parking lot and the Wilderness boundary near the lake's head. Cabins dot the shore, each one built by a private owner on land leased from the Forest Service.

From time to time the region reveals vestiges of true wilderness: a hawk flying close overhead with a chipmunk in its circled talons or the voice of the high country in the boughs of a red fir. Nevertheless, this gateway to Desolation Wilderness everywhere bears witness to the presence of humans. There is none of the feeling of Inyo, the Dwelling Place of a Great Spirit. Desolation is, in fact, a mini-Wilderness, only 15 miles long by six to eight across. The mountains are smaller, softer of mien; the passes lie well below 10,000 feet, and they issue onto land more gentle and inviting than the austere and sometimes forbidding high country to the south. "Desolation Wilderness is too pretty, too nice," says the young ranger who tends it; "and," he adds somewhat ruefully, mindful of its proximity to the residential areas that border Lake Tahoe, "too available."

Because it is so available and so pretty and so small, it has become a kind of back-country pressure cooker wherein the residual problems affecting the whole Sierra wilderness have boiled up into a concentrated and sometimes unhappy stew. Here, as elsewhere in the Sierra, there are simply too many wilderness lovers for the existing terrain to absorb. During the 1979 season, 220,115 people came into Desolation for stays of 12 hours or more—three times the number of such visitors a decade earlier—and very nearly loved the place to death. One day, before a camping permit system was instituted, a young ranger looked down from a ridge onto Lake of the Woods where backpackers' tents were jammed together ridgepole to ridgepole, almost like a Civil War encampment. "This is not wilderness," he said. "This is not what Congress intended."

Nor was the scene on a similar day in the Minarets Wilderness along the shores of Shadow Lake, where no fewer than 450 people had set up their tents, built campfires, and were flailing the small body of water to a froth with their fly lines and spinning outfits. Now only 30 people are permitted to camp each day at the lake. Even the mighty summit of Mount Whitney itself, tallest peak in the Sierra Nevada, is no barrier to the swarm of Sierra visitors. On an average summer weekend 200 people clamber to Whitney's top, clad in everything from bathing suits to

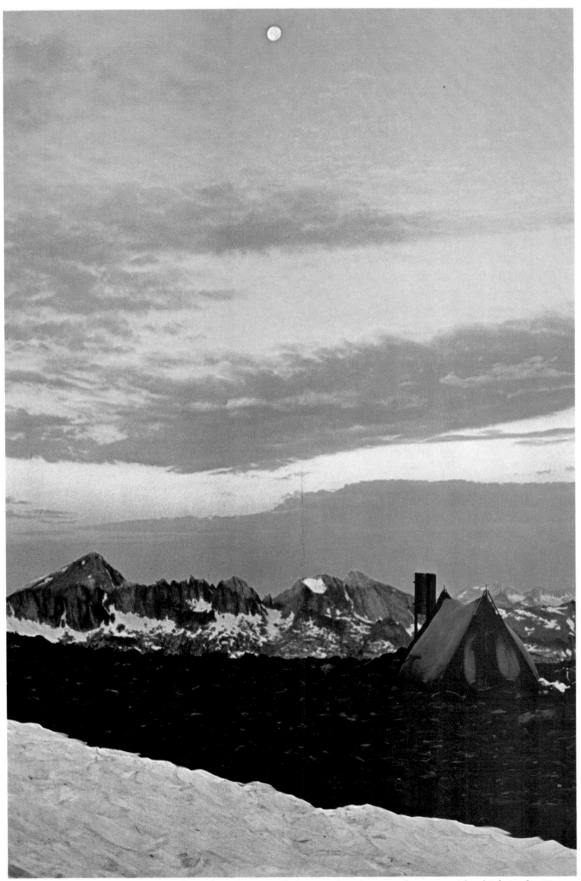

Near twilight, a camper's tent stands anchored to a trail signpost (rear) on a gale-swept ridge high in the Sierra.

the business suit, complete with bow tie and fedora, worn by a natty California hiker who carried his duffel in a suitcase. On another occasion an unidentified pioneer battled to the top pushing a wheelbarrow. Before a quota was imposed to hold down climbers' numbers to 75 a day, 1,500 souls appeared on Whitney's crest one Labor Day, creating such a mess that the rangers had to direct a helicopter to land on the summit and remove the accumulated trash.

There is a reasonable doubt that, in passing the Wilderness Act, Congress intended this sort of thing either.

Even in the fall, long after the crowds have gone, some of the high country retains a frayed and weary look. The John Muir Trail itself, spine of the Sierra wilderness system, is scraped and pounded in some places by horseshoes and hikers' boots into a dusty trough that has sunk two feet below the bordering meadow grass. And on a quiet autumn day at nearby Lake of the Woods, a horseman, dismounted and stretched out to rest by the shore, was harshly awakened by the snap of six rounds of light-caliber rifle fire, followed minutes later by the even booming of nine rounds from a heavier rifle. The sound was especially unsettling to this horseman since only a few years earlier, while topping a neighboring rise, he had heard the snick of a rifle bolt and found himself peering down the muzzle of a weapon held by a drunken deer hunter. "The big question," said the horseman to the ranger, "is how can we use the wilderness and still preserve it? Where a camper used to have the trails to himself, now they're covered with Joe Blow and a million like him. But you can't close off the wilderness. That would defeat the purpose."

The ranger, being young, had a quick and contentious reply. "I don't manage people," he said. "I manage land. And if there is a conflict between land and people, the people have to go."

Hard words, and they are being backed by policy. Nowadays everyone who goes into a Sierra wilderness managed by the Forest Service must obtain a permit on which he states how many are in his party, how long they will stay and where they will enter and exit. Originally intended to provide a count on the numbers of people going into the wilderness, the permits have become a means of protecting the land by limiting visitors—pretty much the way the young ranger told it.

"There are two kinds of wilderness resources we have to protect," explained a manager of the John Muir Wilderness, "the actual physical resource and the more intangible solitude resource. Let's say you could have 100 people in a lake basin at a given time and not hurt the physical resource—but 100 people might hurt the solitude factor. So you'd take a lower figure. At a place like Shadow Lake it's 30. And if someone got there, say, the second week in August and there were already 30 people on the lake, then he'd have to go somewhere else."

With both kinds of resources in mind, rangers have taken additional—and decisive—steps in tailoring people's use of the wilderness to the carrying capacity of the land. In certain parts of the back country, most particularly in Yosemite, Kings Canyon and Sequoia National Parks, a travel group is restricted to a maximum of 25 people. Furthermore, a maximum number of permits, usually 25, has been established for each trailhead. Back-country travelers who arrive after the permit limit has been reached have the option of either accepting a permit that is still available for another route, or cooling their heels—and packs—until the following day.

Another way to manage physical resources, and encourage a sense of solitude as well, is to lay down conditions for campsites. Throughout the Charlotte and Rae Lakes districts of Kings Canyon Park, no one may camp within 100 feet of any stream or lake, or stay more than one night at any given campsite. "This way," explains a ranger, "you don't get those big groups staying forever at one place and making a horrible mess. And by moving 'em back from the water, we cut down the danger of pollution and improve the esthetics. You know how sound carries over water; and you don't want to look across a lake and see 27 other tents on the opposite shore."

One back-country management report has gone so far as to recommend no washing or bathing in natural waterways: "Do you want to be taking a drink from some mountain brook," asks a backpacker, "and here comes the detergent from some guy's week-old socks and underwear floating by?" And since 1960 at the very popular camping area at Bullfrog Lake in Sequoia National Park, where the trail ruts had begun to fork and crisscross like some bucolic freightyard and the tentsites were bare, trampled earth, all camping has been forbidden for an indefinite period to allow the land to restore itself.

The next obvious step—no mater how repulsive it may appear to a people raised in the tradition of free land—is camping by advance reservation. The administrators of Sequoia National Park, to take an example, reserve half the total number of overnight permits allowed for a particular trail on any given date during the summer season. Reservations must be requested, however, before the season gets under way.

Once the rush has commenced, camping permits are issued on a first-come, first-served basis. "The time has passed," mused a ranger solemnly, "when every American can go where he wants, stay as long as he wants, and do what he wants. If he keeps on, we won't have any wilderness left; and that's what we're being paid to preserve."

As an old-line wilderness lover, brought up in a nation created for the very purpose of encouraging everyone to do his thing, I find the notions of restricted camping and reservations revolting. And as a devout horseman I have some dark thoughts about the tight grazing regulations. Yet I concur in them, absolutely. I would rather have my wilderness rationed than not have it at all. And if my horse hurts a meadow by grazing in it before the spring meltwater drains from the marshy areas, then my horse cannot go there, even if spring does not end until August 1—as happens sometimes in the high country after a hard winter.

Thus I find myself in agreement with the general drift of National Park and Forest Service policy to keep us all from loving our wilderness to death. The fact is that the last real Sierra wilderness is already dead, in the sense that there are hardly any remaining virgin spots untrod by human feet and where anyone who comes can be completely alone.

Fortunately there are still quite a few places off the beaten track where the land, though visited before, still fits the words of the Wilderness Act: "retaining its primeval character and influence (and having) outstanding opportunities for solitude." I know of such places, but I am not going to tell you where they are, because then you would come to them and intrude upon my solitude. For the way of mankind is perverse and gregarious. He has legislated Wilderness because in his heart and bones he knows he needs it. But once he enters the wild country he seeks the company of others, bunching up at the better-known campgrounds and hiking only on the main trails.

For such reasons, the Wilderness areas require a high degree of management by the custodians, and a high degree of restraint upon the part of the visitors. Both are necessary, for while the outlook for wilderness is good, and the old, exploitative enemies of the wild country have been mostly held in check, most of us have failed to take note of the rise of the ultimate enemy to the sanctity of the Sierra. As the comic-strip character Pogo once said in a flash of brilliantly illuminated irony, "We have met the enemy and he is us."

Of course no one, and particularly no member of the Sierra Club or any other such passionate organization, wants to think of himself as the worst enemy the wilderness ever had. But a few of them are and certainly together we all are, so long as we try to go wherever we want, stay as long as we want and insist on doing whatever we want. Fortunately, most people are beginning to understand and to adjust to the concept of managed wilderness. Though they may concede the necessity of some of the things the wilderness custodians are doing to keep us lovers decently at bay (e.g., party limits, camping reservations), they remain confused about or ill-disposed toward some of the others. One is manipulation of the fish population. I happen to go into the wilderness for solitude and, incidentally, to fish. But, says one Forest Service administrator, "part of our problem is that a lot of people are coming here *just* to fish. And they don't care if they're in wilderness; they carry out their quota of fish just the same. So maybe we're going to have to limit fish planting."

"It gets down to this," said one California Fish and Game man, "and the decision goes way beyond just fishing into the whole question of wilderness use: do we want to have the real Wilderness that Congress legislated, where we manage for solitude and try to maintain a natural state of things? Or do we encourage things like fish planting to provide a recreational experience for masses of people?"

The question of hunting is just as difficult. Says one forest supervisor, "*Overnight* I'd like to eliminate firearms from the wilderness in summer." So would every single ranger and honest sportsman in the Sierra. Guns are scary to a lot of people; besides, there is no excuse for using them on songbirds, squirrels or marmots. But legitimate hunting for designated game animals in season is a far different story. For while it is pleasant to think theoretically of the wilderness as a wildlife sanctuary, more than a century of hunting has reshuffled the relationships of the Sierra's animals to one another. Many of the predators have been killed off. Without them, populations of the herbivorous animals such as deer tend to expand to unhealthy dimensions. In the parks, where hunting has always been prohibited, rangers periodically shoot dozens of mule deer from swollen herds that have overrun the available browse. To keep the herds down all over the wilderness, supervised hunters—perhaps with restricted permits rather than unlimited licenses—could shoot this surplus.

Conflict springs from other kinds of wilderness use, creating nagging questions of safety and convenience that the wilderness managers are struggling to solve—or at least cope with. The most dramatic is the problem of keeping mountain climbers from killing themselves and risking the lives of large teams of volunteer rescuers. On a warm May morning not long ago five men clad in light pants and thin jackets started up Mount Ritter in the Minarets Wilderness. By midafternoon a blizzard had closed down on them, with winds of 60 to 70 miles per hour; next day four of the five were dead of exposure while some two dozen hikers and helicopter-borne rescuers scoured the mountains for the lone survivor. "The Sierra is very unforgiving," said a ranger, "if you don't respect its hazards."

Some of the Sierra's custodians are unforgiving too, and with reason. For 27 days in the fall of 1970, two widely publicized rock climbers hammered and clawed their way up the sheer southeast face of El Capitan in Yosemite as a rescue team of 18 other mountaineers waited to find out whether they would have to put their own necks on the line should the adventurers fail to reach the summit safely (they eventually made it). "Why the hell didn't they just climb the Empire State Building?" asked one veteran ranger who, like most other officials, saw the climb not as derring-do but a tiresome ego exercise that cost the Park Service a lot of time and worry, and could have cost lives as well. "If people go into the back country to climb or take other risks," he continued, "they should be able to get themselves out."

Danger, and the willingness of each person to deal with it, are legitimate parts of the wilderness experience. But at the same time, everyone, including that hard-nosed official, privately concedes you cannot leave a trapped climber to rot on the end of his rope or tell an imprudent hiker's family you don't care that he froze to death. Thus normal rescue operations will continue in the wilderness, just as they do on public beaches. However, for high-risk adventures such as the El Capitan climb, it is perfectly reasonable, as several rangers have urged, to require mountaineers to bring their own backup rescue teams or otherwise satisfy the local wilderness authority that they have the experience and equipment for the ascent they are attempting.

On other, less spectacular aspects of wilderness administration the logic of evolving policies, however virtuous their intent, remains muddled. For example, the Wilderness Act specifies "the imprint of man's work [shall be] substantially unnoticeable." Yet some wilderness managers have installed such semicivilized amenities as latrines in the wilderness—"not as a convenience but to protect the ecology," as one ranger explained it.

Both the forest and park officials are still building and maintaining bridges over certain dangerous streams that cannot be safely forded on

The parallel gashes marring this alpine meadow may be the ruts of bygone mining or logging roads deepened by decades of horses' hoofs and hikers' feet. The meadows here are fragile because of the short summer at these altitudes. The soil remains moist and the grasses never root deeply. When vehicles, animals and hikers use the same path, they form a rut that becomes even deeper, often beyond repair, when eroded by frequent summer showers.

foot or horseback, and where no alternate route is reasonably available.

On the other hand they have taken several other measures so pure that even some purists are complaining. Existing trails are being allowed to erode away in some parts of the wilderness, and in other parts they are being rerouted away from damaged meadows until the fragile sod can recover. The number of horses is now also restricted on many trails, and it would startle no one if they were barred altogether from areas where the maintenance required for livestock passage is unreasonable. Desolation, for example, is a Wilderness so small that horses conflict with hikers on the trails and campsites.

The managers responsible for making and enforcing rules like these do so with one eye cocked on practical matters and the other scanning the wording of the laws that created their jobs. The conscientious effort this takes deserves credit. But paradoxically, hard, earnest work along such lines, carried out over a period of years, can create dilemmas never imagined either by legislators or managers. There is one problem, for instance, that the National Park Service has just barely begun to resolve: Is a park a natural museum or a national resort? When Congress first established the park system it laid down a mandate for the Service "to conserve the scenery and the natural . . . objects and the wild life therein and to provide for the enjoyment of the same in such manner and by such means as will leave them unimpaired for the enjoyment of future generations." Since then park personnel have generally been more zealous about providing for the public's enjoyment of the scenery and natural objects, and about conserving everything in sight, than they have been about leaving the place unimpaired. As a result large areas in the parks, particularly in Yosemite and in parts of Kings Canyon and Sequoia, became unhappy hybrids, something between woodsy resorts and glorified zoos.

Yosemite, for example, has two hotels (with wire fences to keep deer out of the flower gardens), four swimming pools, five grocery and general stores, five souvenir shops, two golf courses, six gas stations, a bank, a post office, a coin-operated laundry, a small emergency hospital handling a brisk turnover of traffic casualties, regulated campsites on the valley floor for 6,000 people, an elaborate dude stable affiliated with a string of wooden-floored campsites for another 2,400 people and a vast motel complex that does a thriving trade with business convention-eers when not otherwise crowded to the eaves with ordinary tourists.

On a big holiday weekend up to 40,000 souls jam into the valley, trailing candy wrappers and carbon monoxide gas. And at such times, with excursionists tumbling out of buses and motorcyclists blasting around, Yosemite can take on the air of an extravagant Hollywood aberration, as if D. W. Griffith had created the setting and had then left the rest to a mad director with a cast of all the wrong thousands. A dismal nadir occurred during the Fourth of July weekend in 1970, when a mounted troop of 16 rangers, augmented by a foot patrol of 21, charged a meadow full of stoked-up, bongo-drumming young people. The result was the first riot in national park history. Wielding lassoes, clubs, handcuffs and Mace, the rangers arrested 186 and left a rotten taste in everyone's mouths, including their own. The legacy of that unhappy episode was that the image of park ranger changed temporarily from earnest custodian of the forest to "tree pig"—the coinage of one furious youngster— and the image of Yosemite to Woodstock West. Nobody was more aware of the change or more dismayed than the rangers themselves, one of whom resigned outright while others commented grimly that they hadn't joined the park rangers to be policemen.

Fortunately both for present images and the future security of Yosemite, the National Park Service has taken several giant steps toward cutting down both the congestion and the confusion in the valley—and eventually toward getting Yosemite out of the resort business altogether. Beginning around the time of the riot, automobiles and all other private vehicles were permanently barred from the east end of the valley, and the road system recast into a series of one-way loops that tended to make frustrated motorists wish they had left their vehicles at home. And that was precisely the point. "The most jarring thing in Yosemite has been the cars," says the man directly responsible for valley administration. "After all, you're not allowed to drive your car through the Smithsonian," adds a ranger. Little by little, Yosemite has substituted comfortable shuttle buses for private automobiles with remarkably positive results.

As early as the autumn after the riot, the closed parking lots in the east end were covered with carpets of pine needles, disturbed only by occasional strollers. The following July, though the visitor count for the month had increased from the riot year, most people chose to leave their cars in the remaining parking lots and to walk around the valley. As a crowd they seemed much quieter and more attuned to the real beauty of Yosemite, and the valley itself seemed to be recapturing a sense of peace that it had lost too long ago. "It was so quiet," said one weekend visitor, "I thought maybe this was the way it was before people came to Yosemite." To assure a permanent change for the better, the park people will be guided in the future by a master plan, adopted in 1980, that fully involves the public in all phases of decision-making.

To make the new plan really succeed, however, the Park Service has to complete another giant step, this one away from its old habit of preserving natural things at the expense of natural processes. For years the service saw its parks as an aggregate of things—trees, deer and the like. And protection of these things became almost an obsession. No tree could burn, even if the threatening fire came from a source as natural as lightning. In fact the obsession became so complete that for a time it appeared no tree, however old, would even be permitted to fall: one survey recommended attaching guy wires to a huge sequoia nicknamed the Grizzly Giant to prevent it from toppling over, as nature clearly intended it would one day.

As a result of being protected from the natural processes out of which it had evolved, the character of the park wilderness began to change. Lodgepole pines invaded many of the meadows, which had been cleared by periodic fires before the coming of the preservationists, and thick stands of fire-protected white fir and incense cedar began to crowd in on the great sequoias, filling up the open spaces their tiny seeds need in order to germinate.

"This kind of fire protection has been a doomsday route," said a ranger. "By eliminating any fire you change the composition of the forest. You get what we've got here now, which is a building of underbrush and fuel that could set off a real wildfire." The parks are beginning to correct this unnatural situation through selective clearing, and by the deliberate setting of controlled, small-radius fires that allow the proper balance of forest growth to regenerate. After that, natural fires will be permitted to reassert the logic of their own control.

At the same time the managers of the parks are taking a hard look at their tendency to overprotect such creatures as deer, and at their practice of introducing other soft-eyed forest denizens simply to have them around. Several years ago a colony of beaver, previously alien to the High Sierra, was planted in parts of the Kern River region in Sequoia Park. "Gosh, you couldn't say enough good about the beaver—we thought," sighed one ranger. "Cute, nature's little engineers, all that. But then they started cutting down trees and damming streams, deteriorating the golden trout habitat so the fish couldn't spawn. And now we're faced with the job of taking out the beaver. We really screwed up there."

"I think you've got to figure," said another, "that any ecosystem has developed over hundreds of thousands of years; and through evolution there is a balance between animals and vegetation. And once we break the glass, we have a lot of trouble putting the pieces back together. If we wipe out the grizzly or the condor, we can't really put them back —not the native animals, anyway. We've made some awful mistakes. And after a while it gets to be a zoo kind of thing, putting animals in there that don't belong."

Managing the animals that do belong can get to be a "zoo thing" that tampers with natural processes, and that tendency is being questioned, too. For in a park, as in any wilderness, it is a contradiction in terms for a visitor to be able to go to Point A with a guarantee of seeing a deer, or to Point B for a pine marten. Rather, such an encounter should be a chance one, as it has always been in nature. You should go into the wilderness simply to be there. And if you are very lucky, you may see a pine marten. And then, if you care, you can learn about it and its ways, how it relates to the land and the climate and they to it. And the next time you see one or read or hear of one, the experience will be a deeper one. And you yourself will feel a singleness with the pine marten, for that is what you are—simply another creature who is a significant and yet insignificant part of the land and the air, the soil and the climate, the animals and the forest. And then, perhaps for the first time in your life, you may truly begin to know something about yourself and your world. And that is what the wilderness is all about.

Discovery of a Living Valley

PHOTOGRAPHS BY HARALD SUND

Most visitors to Yosemite see the valley as a spectacle—huge in scale, full of brilliant light, dominated by towering rocks and leaping waterfalls. This is the awe-inspiring Yosemite, often described as timeless and enduring, a monument to the age of the glaciers. Hidden within it, visible to only a few, is another Yosemite, mysterious, vital, constantly changing, all unaware of the monumental role ascribed to it.

This is the Yosemite that intrigued photographer Harald Sund and became the subject of the pictures on the following pages. To discover it, Sund, who had never been there before, immersed himself in Yosemite, studying the details of the valley as well as its entirety, observing it by moonlight as well as in full sun. "Actually," he says, "I photographed the valley in my mind. Then I came back with the camera."

For Sund, the shot of El Capitan's granitic flank (opposite), with the chip of rock in the foreground, brings the scale of the valley down to manageable proportion by contrasting the detail with the vast sweep of rock in the background. In making the picture of dewdrops sparkling on the grass of Leidig Meadow (pages 174-175), he was try-ing to offset the restful quality of the meadow's flat, green surface against the vertical harshness of the surrounding cliffs. The strange nighttime softness of Lower Yosemite Falls (page 176) dramatizes Sund's feeling of wonder that the water—seemingly so pliant—could carve the unyielding rock.

Inevitably, Sund could not transfer all of his perceptions onto film. He had to forgo a splendid shot of lightning striking Half Dome when his own position, on the tip of Glacier Point, became a storm target. A rare lunar rainbow, caused by moonlight on spray from a waterfall, eluded him when his film proved unequal to the task of catching the spectral colors.

Generally, however, Sund managed to record things that the average visitor seldom sees: sunlight piercing the leaves of a dogwood grove ("The eye resists looking directly into the sun, but the camera doesn't flinch"), clouds shadowed by other clouds, the thrust of a tree root against a boulder. To Sund, all these speak of mysteries awaiting discovery, of a valley still in flux, an unfinished product. Far from being a memorial to the geological past, Sund's Yosemite is very much alive.

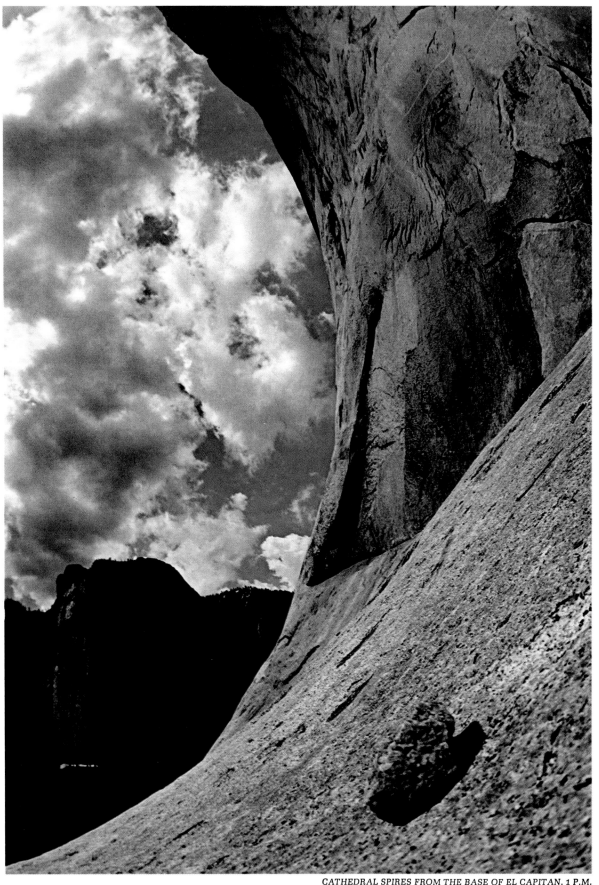

CATHEDRAL SPIRES FROM THE BASE OF EL CAPITAN, 1 P.M.

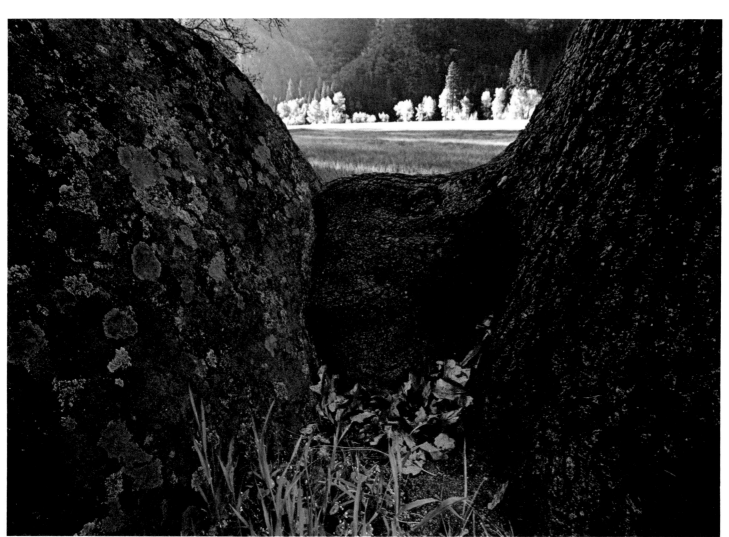

ROCK AND OAK: LEIDIG MEADOW, 7:30 A.M.

BRIDALVEIL FALL, 5:30 A.M.

SUNRISE OVER HALF DOME FROM LEIDIG MEADOW, 7:30 A.M.

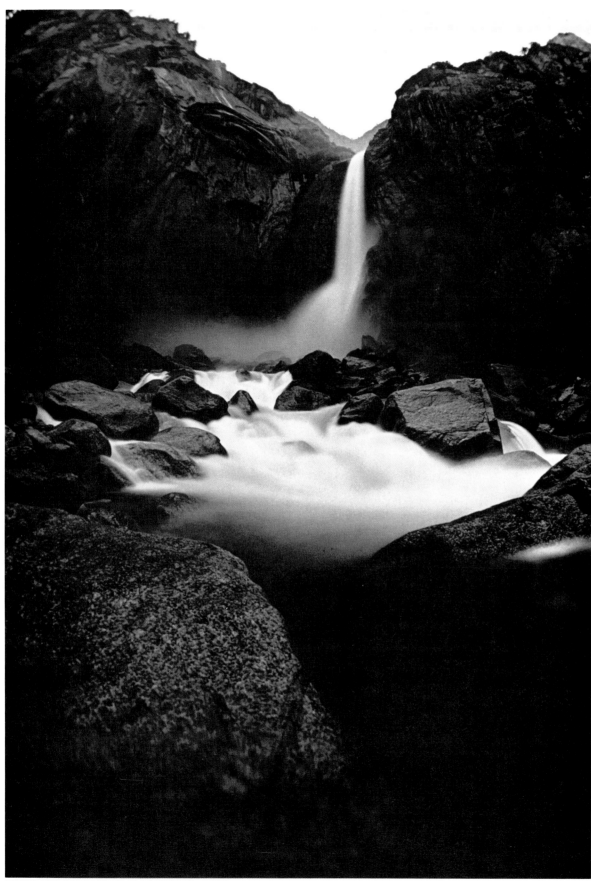

LOWER YOSEMITE FALLS AT NIGHTFALL, 9 P.M.

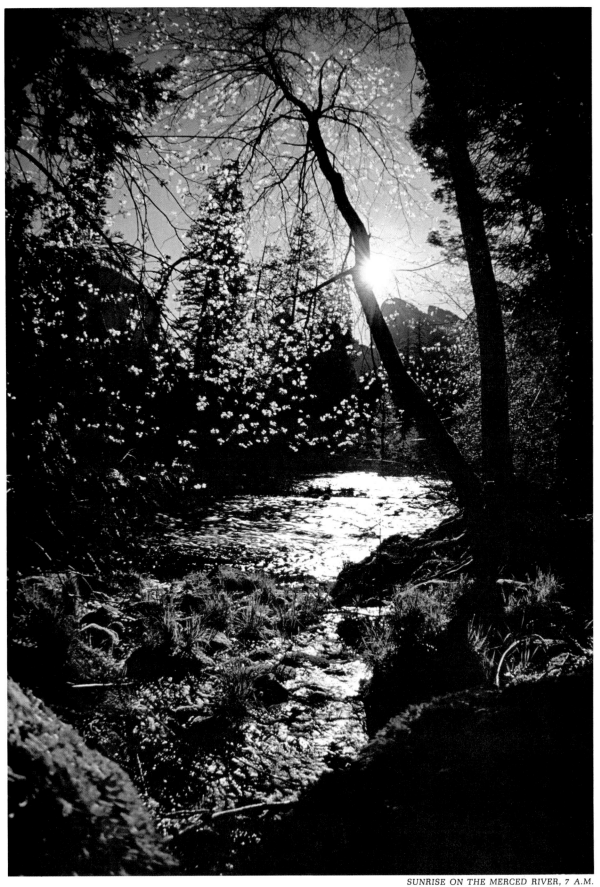

SUNRISE ON THE MERCED RIVER, 7 A.M.

CLARK RANGE AND HALF DOME FROM GLACIER POINT, 8:30 P.M.

Acknowledgments

The author and editors of *The High Sierra* are indebted to Genny Schumacher Smith, Palo Alto, California, and Sidney S. Horenstein, Department of Invertebrate Paleontology, The American Museum of Natural History, New York City. They also wish to thank: Paul Bateman, U.S. Geological Survey; Harold H. Biswell, Professor of Forestry, University of California, Berkeley; Gordon Boyd, Sequoia and Kings Canyon National Parks; B. K. Cooperrider, U.S. Forest Service; David J. Dunaway, Inyo National Forest; Dan Farris, Mammoth Lakes, California; Miklos Faust, U.S. Department of Agriculture, Beltsville Research Center, Maryland; Coyt H. Hackett, Yosemite National Park; Bryan Harry, Yosemite National Park; Glenn Haas, Forest Service, Washington, D.C.; John Thomas Howell, Curator Emeritus, Department of Botany, California Academy of Sciences, San Francisco; William C. Jones, Three Rivers, California; Charles R. Joy, Forest Service, Washington, D.C.; Bruce Kilgore, Sequoia and Kings Canyon National Parks; Lee W. Lenz, Director, Rancho Santa Ana Botanic Garden, Claremont, California; A. Starker Leopold, Professor of Zoology, University of California, Berkeley; Elizabeth McClintock, California Academy of Sciences, San Francisco; Ronald J. McCormick, Inyo National Forest; John McLaughlin, Superintendent, Sequoia and Kings Canyon National Parks; Woodrow W. Middlecauff, Professor of Entomology, University of California, Berkeley; Duncan Morrow, National Park Service, Washington, D.C.; Lawrence S. Nahm, Yosemite National Park; James M. Olsen, Eldorado National Forest; Larry Pardue, The New York Botanical Garden, New York City; Philip Pister, California Department of Fish and Game; Leo Porterfield, Inyo National Forest; Elizabeth Potts, San Francisco, California; Douglas Powell, Berkeley, California; Joseph T. Radel, Bishop, California; James I. Reveal, Assistant Professor of Botany, University of Maryland; Richard Riegelhuth, Sequoia and Kings Canyon National Parks; Edwin C. Rockwell, Inyo National Forest; Arnold P. Snyder, Sierra National Forest; Edward C. Stone, Professor of Forestry, University of California, Berkeley; Jan Studebaker, Yosemite Park and Curry Company; Clyde Wahrhaftig, Professor of Geology, University of California, Berkeley; Joseph Wampler, Berkeley, California; Robert S. Wood, Berkeley, California.

Bibliography

Best, Gerald M., *Snowplow: Clearing Mountain Rails.* Howell-North, 1966.

Brewer, William H., *Up and Down California in 1860-1864.* University of California Press, 1966.

Brown, Vinson, *The Reading Woods.* Stackpole Books, 1969.

Brown, Vinson, and Robert Livezey, *The Sierra Nevadan Wildlife Region.* Naturegraph Company, 1962.

Dobie, J. Frank, *The Voice of the Coyote.* University of Nebraska Press, 1961.

Farquhar, Francis P., *History of the Sierra Nevada.* University of California Press, 1969.

Johnston, Hank, *They Felled the Redwoods.* Trans-Anglo Books, 1966.

Johnston, Verna R., *Sierra Nevada.* Houghton Mifflin Company, 1970.

Landi, Val, *The Bantam Great Outdoors Guide to the United States and Canada.* Bantam Books, Inc., 1978.

Little, Elbert L., *The Audubon Society Field Guide to North American Trees Western Region.* Alfred A. Knopf, 1980.

Matthes, François E., *The Incomparable Valley.* University of California Press, 1970.

Matthews, William H., III, *A Guide to the National Parks: Vol. I, The Western Parks.* Natural History Press, 1968.

Muir, John, *The Mountains of California.* Natural History Books, 1961.

Muir, John, and Richard Kauffman, *Gentle Wilderness.* Sierra Club-Ballantine Books, 1968.

Munz, Philip A., *California Mountain Wildflowers.* University of California Press, 1969.

Nash, Roderick, *Wilderness and the American Mind.* Yale University Press, 1967.

National Geographic Society, *The New America's Wonderlands.* 1980.

Press, Frank and Raymond Siever, *Earth.* W. H. Freeman and Company, 1978.

Roth, Hal, *Pathway in the Sky: The Story of the John Muir Trail.* Howell-North, 1965.

Russell, Carl P., *100 Years in Yosemite.* Yosemite Natural History Assn., 1968.

Schumacher, Genny, ed., *Deepest Valley.* Wilderness Press, 1969.

Schumacher, Genny, ed., *The Mammoth Lakes Sierra.* Wilderness Press, 1969.

Schwenke, Karl, and Thomas Winnett, *Sierra North.* Wilderness Press, 1967.

Schwenke, Karl, and Thomas Winnett, *Sierra South.* Wilderness Press, 1968.

Starr, Walter A., Jr., *Starr's Guide: Guide to the John Muir Trail and the High Sierra Region.* Sierra Club, 1970.

Storer, Tracy I., and Robert L. Usinger, *Sierra Nevada Natural History.* University of California Press, 1968.

Picture Credits

Sources for pictures in this book are shown below. Credits for pictures from left to right are separated by commas, from top to bottom by dashes.

COVER–Jack H. Lawrence. Front end papers 1, 2–Harald Sund. End paper 3, page 1–Martin Litton. 2, 3–John O. Beahrs. 4, 5–Don Carlson. 6, 7–Jack H. Lawrence. 8, 9–David Muench. 10, 11–Harald Sund. 12, 13–Sonja Bullaty. 18-19–Map by R. R. Donnelley Cartographic Services.

CHAPTER 1: 23–David Muench. 28, 29 –David Muench. 35–From *John of the Mountains* by Linnie Marsh Wolfe, 1938, Houghton Mifflin Co., Boston. 36 –Courtesy of the Bancroft Library. 37 –Robert A. Weinstein. 38, 39–Courtesy of the Bancroft Library. 40, 41 –Harold G. Schutt courtesy Tulare County Historical Society. 42, 43–Collection Roy D. Graves courtesy Gerald M. Best. 44–National Park Service. 45 –Courtesy History Archives, Los Angeles County Museum of Natural History. 46, 47–Joseph Le Conte courtesy Sierra Club.

CHAPTER 2: 50, 51–W. C. Mendenhall courtesy U. S. Geological Survey. 56, 57 –Frank Lerner. 65–Harald Sund. 66, 67–Sonja Bullaty. 68, 69, 70–David Muench. 71–Philip Hyde.

CHAPTER 3: 79–David Muench. 84–Angelo Lomeo. 85–Richard C. Burns except top left Sonja Bullaty. 89 through 103–Sonja Bullaty and Angelo Lomeo.

CHAPTER 4: 107–Kenneth W. Fink. 110 –Kenneth W. Fink. 112–Ronn Patterson–Tom Tracy from PhotoFind, Ed Park. 113–Ronn Patterson. 115– Hal Roth. 116, 117–Kenneth W. Fink, Maurice G. Hornocker. 120–David J. Dunaway. 124 through 135–David Cavagnaro.

CHAPTER 5: 140, 141, 143–Sonja Bullaty. 147–George Silk for LIFE magazine. 148, 149–George Silk for LIFE magazine except center Edward S. Ross. 150, 151–George Silk for LIFE magazine. 152, 153–David Cavagnaro except bottom right Tom Myers. 154, 155 –Sonja Bullaty.

CHAPTER 6: 160–George Silk for LIFE magazine. 165–Sue Rayfield. 171 through 179–Harald Sund.

Index

Numerals in italics indicate a photograph
or drawing of the subject mentioned.

A

Abbot, Mount, 74
Alabama Hills, *28-29*
Alpine Meadows, 137
Alta Morris Lake, 104
American Journal of Science, 61
American River, 34, 55
Anne Lake, 49, 51, 74
Army Pass, old and new, 21, 32
Ashburner, William, *39*
Avalanches, 42, 83, 140
Averell, Chester, *39*

B

Bark structure and texture, 83, *84-85,* 94
Bartholomew, Orland, 140, 144
Bats, 132, 146
Baxter, Mount, 120
Beaver, 113, 168
Bee fly, *128,* 129
Big Oak Flat Road, 44
Big Whitney Meadow, 140
Blueberry, dwarf, 132
Brewer, William H., *39,* 72
Bridalveil Fall, *57, 173*
Buckbrush, 86
Buckwheat, 132
Bullfrog Lake, 162
Butterfly, Behr's sulphur *(Colias behrii),*
   126

C

Caddis fly, 114, 127, 129
Calaveras Skull, 61-62
California Geological Survey, members, *39*
Camas, 99
Camping. *See* Tourism
Canadian Zone, 88, *98-99*
Cascade Valley, 53
Cathedral Spires, *171*
Cedar, incense, 168
Chagoopa Plateau, 22
Chaparral, 86, 90
Charlotte Lake, 162
Cherokee Flat, California, 61
Chickadee, 139
Chipmunk, 138; alpine *(Eutamias*

alpinus), 75, 86, 113, 132, *133*
Cinquefoil, yellow *(Potentilla glandulosa),*
   150-151
City of San Francisco (train), 140
Clark Range, *178-179*
Cliff-brake fern *(Pellaea bridgesii), 153*
Climate and weather, 21, 23, 56, 83, 90, 94,
   98, 100, 131, 139-140, 136-146. *See also*
   Life zones
Clover, mustang *(Linanthus montanus),*
   96; owl *(Orthocarpus erianthus), 91*
Columbine, 132; yellow alpine *(Aquilegia*
   pubescens), 102-103, 132
Congress Grove, *8-9*
Conservation measures, 26-28, 77-78, 156-
   169
Cottonwood Canyon, 20-22, *32-33*
Cottonwood Creek, 20
Cottonwood Lakes, 21, 23, 115, 118
Cougar *(Felis concolor),* 80, 105, *116-117*
Coyote *(Canis latrans),* 80, 104-106, *107,*
   108-110, 138, 144
Crabtree Meadow, 137, 139
Currant, gooseberry, 132

D

Davis Strait, 72
Deer, 80-81, 117, 138
Desolation Wilderness, 104, *158-159,* 166
Devils Postpile, *23*
Devon Island, 76
Disney Productions, 157
Domes, 64, *66-67*
Donner, George, and party, 25, 140
Donner Pass, 26, *42-43*
Donner Summit, 142
Douglas, William O., 48
Duck Lake, 72, 76, 78
Duck Pass, 72, 74

E

Eagle, 138
Eagle Peak (Rock), 56, *58-59*
Earthquake of 1872, 51, 58
Echo Lake, 32, *158-159*
El Capitan, 23, 56, 165, 170, *171*
Elephant heads, 132
Elizabeth Pass, *154-155*
Emerson, Ralph Waldo, 27-28
Emigrant Gap, 42
Erosion, 51-52, 56, 59-60, 64, 68-71, 124

Erratics, 51, *68*
Evolution. *See* Geology and evolution
Evolution Creek, 124, 131
Exfoliation, *66-67*
Exploitation. *See* Conservation measures

F

Farewell-to-spring *(Clarkia viminea),* 90,
   91
Fiesta flower *(Pholistoma auritum), 91*
Filaree, *93*
Finch, rosy, 139
Fir: red *(Abies magnifica),* 85, 88, *98;*
   white *(Abies concolor),* 94, *140-141,* 168
Fires, effect on ecology, 86, 168
Fish, 77-78, 139, 164. *See also by name*
Fish Creek, 72, 74, 77, 81, 83, 87
Five-spot *(Nemophila maculata), 93*
Flax blue *(Linum perenne), 154, 155*
Flowers, wild, endpaper 3, page 1. *See*
   also by name
Fly, bee, *128,* 129; crane, *132*
Font, Fray Pedro, 25
Frémont, John Charles, 25, 140
Fringepod *(Thysanocarpus curvipes), 93*
Frog, yellow-legged *(Rana muscosa),* 127,
   130, 131
Fungus, train-wrecker *(Lentinus lepideus),*
   126, *127*

G

Gabb, William More, *39*
Geology and evolution, 25-26, 48-55, *56-*
   57, 58, 64, *65-71*
Geranium, cranesbill *(Geranium*
   richardsonii), 97
Giant Forest, 24, 29
Glacier Point, 23, *178-179*
Glaciers, and effects of, *2-3, 23,* 48, *50-51,*
   56-57, 60-62, 64, *68-71,* 77, *130-131, 133*
Gold, discovery and mining of, 27, 34, *36-*
   37, 55, 157. *See also* Mining
Gophers, pocket, 113, 144
Great Western Divide, *12-13,* 23
Grouse, Sierra, 145

H

Half Dome, 23, 49, 56, *57,* 60, 62, 64, *65,*
   170, *174-175, 178-179*
Harte, Bret, 61, 136
Harvard University, 61

Hawk, Cooper, 75, 127-128, 138
Heather, red (Phyllodoce breweri), 77, 100
Heavenly Valley, 137
Helianthella (Helianthella californica), 97
Hemlock, 76
Hetch Hetchy Valley, 34
Hicks, Edward, 138
High Sierra Trail, 29-30
Hilgard, Mount, 74
Hoffmann, Charles F., 38-39
Horse riding, 81-82, 166
Hudsonian Zone, 88, 100-101
Hunting, control of, 164-165
Huxley, Mount, 133

I

Illilouette Basin, 62
Inyo, 72-87
Inyo National Forest, 73, 120, 123
Italy, Lake, 74

J

Jack rabbit, white-tailed, 144
Jointing, 64, 70-71
Junco, 86
Junction Ridge, 22
Juniper (Juniperus occidentalis), 78, 79, 82-83

K

Kaweah Canyon, 24
Kaweah Peaks, 22, 33, 54
Kaweah River, 23
Kern Canyon, 22
Kern Plateau, 26, 115, 118
Kern River, 114, 168
King, Clarence, 39
Kings Canyon National Park, 26, 28-29, 74, 157, 162, 166
Kings River, 22
Kipling, Rudyard, 105

L

Lacepod (Thysanocarpus curvipes), 93
Ladybird beetle, 148-149
Langley, Mount, 22
Larkspur, 97
Lassen Peak, 25
Le Conte Falls, 4-5
Leidig Meadow, 170-172, 174-175
Lichen, 133

Life zones, 88, 89; Arctic-Alpine, 102-103;
Canadian, 98-99; Hudsonian, 100-101;
Transition, 94-97; Upper Sonoran, 90-93
Lily: corn (Veratrum californicus), 98, 99,
126, 146; mariposa (Calochortus
monophyllus), 97, 146, 152, 153; tiger,
98, 99
Livestock grazing, 27, 34, 158
Logging, 27-28, 34, 40-41, 158
Long Pine, California, 58-59
Long Valley, 58
Lower McGee Lake, 134-135
Lower Yosemite Falls, 170, 176
Lumber industry. See Logging
Lupine, 95, 132

M

McGee Canyon, 124, 129
McGee Creek, 124-125, 127-131, 132-133,
134-135
McGee Lakes, 124, 130, 133, 134-135. See
also Lower McGee Lake
McGee, Mount, 133
Malakoff mine, 36, 37
Mammoth Creek, 81
Mammoth Lakes, 72, 77
Mammoth Mountain, 22, 55, 58, 137, 142,
158
Manzanita, 86
Mapping, 34, 38, 39
Marmot (Marmota flaviventris), 112, 113
Marshall, James W., 55
Marten, pine, 144-145
Matthes, Francois, 56
Mayfly, 126, 153
Meadow Lake, 140
Merced River, 23, 56, 177
Mice, grasshopper, 113
Minarets, 2-3, 22, 54
Minarets Wilderness, 159, 165
Mineral King Valley, 157
Miner's lettuce (Montia perfoliata), 92
Mining, 34, 36-37, 157. See also Gold
Mirror Lake, 10-11
Mojave, 25
Monkey flowers, 146; yellow (Mimulus
guttatus), 99
Mosquito, 130, 131
Moss, polytrighum, 125, 126
Mountain lion (Felix concolor), 116-117.
See also Cougar

Mountain misery (Chamaebatia foliolosa),
94, 96
Mountain pride, 129
Muir, John, 20, 27-28, 34, 35, 58-62, 72, 94,
104, 145, 158
Muir Trail, 29, 32, 124, 158, 161
Muir Wilderness, 72-87, 161
Mushroom (Lentinus lepideus), 126, 127

N

National Forest Service, 28, 73-74, 77, 80,
109, 118, 157-159, 161, 163
National Park Service, 28, 109, 137, 157,
163, 166-168
Newt, 153
Nutcracker, Clark (Nucifraga columbiana),
128

O

Oak, live, 90, 172
Olson, Sigurd F., 156
Onion, wild, 77, 126
Ouzel, water (Cinclus mexicanus), 28, 110,
111
Owens River, 58
Owens Valley, 20, 50, 50-51, 58-59, 136

P

Paintbrush, Indian, 77, 100, 101, 154
Parsnip, cow (Heracleum lanatum), 96
Peaceable Kingdom (Hicks painting),
138
Penck, Albrecht, 49
Penstemon: Newberry, 129; whorled, 33
Peter Pande Lake, 53
Phlox, prickly (Leptodactylon pungens),
102
Pika (Ochotona princeps), 75, 112, 113
Pine: digger, 90; Jeffrey (Pinus jeffreyi), 83,
85, 86; knobcone, 86; lodgepole (Pinus
murrayana), 76, 83, 85, 88, 98, 124-125,
168; sugar (Pinus lambertiana), 85, 88;
Western white (Pinus monticola), 84,
85; whitebark (Pinus albicaulis), 74, 76,
100, 101, 128, 133; yellow (Pinus
ponderosa), 84, 85, 88, 94-95
Pine cone, whitebark, 128
Plants. See Vegetation; also by name
Pogo (comic-strip character), 163
Poppy, California (Eschscholtzia
californica), 92

Porcupine, 113
Purple Lake, 83
Pyramid Peak, 26

Q

Quarrying, *70-71*

R

Rae Lake, 162
Railroads, *42-43*
Range of Light, 72
Red Cones, 52
Redtails, 138
Ritter, Mount, 165
Roads and trails, 25-26, 29-31, 44-45, 72-
    73, 82-87, 123, 136, 157-159, *165*, 166-
    167
Rock Creek, 22, *23*, 114
Rock formations and movements, 22, *23*,
    50-51, 52-54, 64, 82, *102-103, 130-131,
    172*
Rockfringe *(Epilobium abcordatum)*, 88,
    102
Roosevelt, Theodore, 28, 117
Roseroot, Western *(Sedum rosea)*, *101*
Royal Arches, 67
Russell, Mount, 33

S

Safety measures, 165
San Joaquin River and Valley, 23, 124
Sawfly, *131*
Saxifrage *(Saxifraga oregana)*, 76, *99*
Sentinel Rock, 23
Sequoia(s): bark, 24, *84*; logging and other
    uses, *40-41; Sequoia gigantea, 8-9*, 24,
    84, 86, 94, 168; *Sequoia sempervirens*,
    24
Sequoia National Park, 26, 28, 34, 123,
    140-141, 143, 149, 154-155, 157, *162-
    163*, 166, 168
Shadow Lake, 159, 162
Sheep, California bighorn *(Ovis
    canadensis)*, *118-119, 120*, 121-123

Shooting star, 94, *95*, 126, *134*, 146
Sierra Club, 34, *46-47*, 157
Sierra Nevada, *map 18-19*; eastern flank,
    50-51
Silver Divide, 49
Simpson Meadow, 74
Sky pilot, 146
Snake, garter *(Thamnophis sirtalis), 127,*
    128
Snow, and hazards of, 21, 23, 26, *42-43*, 55,
    98, *106, 116-117,* 136-138, *140-143,* 145-
    146, *148*
Snowbrush, 138
Snow plant *(Sarcodes sanguinea), 98-99,*
    146, *149*
Sparrow, mountain, 13, 132
Squaw Valley, 137
Squirrels, 138, 145; Belding ground
    (Citellus beldingi), 113; California
    ground *(Citellus beecheyi), 112;*
    Douglas, 145; flying, 113
Stewart, Mount, 24, *88*
Stonecrop, Sierra *(Sedum obtusatum), 100*
Sugar Bowl, 137
Sund, Harald, 170-179
Sutter, John A., 55
Swamp whitehead *(Sphenosciadium
    capitellatum), 125*
Sycamore, California *(Platanus racemosa),*
    90-91

T

Tahoe, Lake, 25, 58
Tamarack, 55
Tertiary Gravels of the Sierra Nevada, 62
Thistle, *152-153*
Thoreau, Henry David, 27-28, 137
Timber line, *6-7*
Timothy grass *(Phleum alpinum), 147*
Tioga Pass, 137
Tourism, and rules for, 26, 29-32, 42, 44,
    74, 77, 80, 123-124, 163, 166-168
Transition Zone, 88, *94-97*
Trout, 138; brook, 77-78, 87; golden

(Salmo aguabonita), 21, 77, 111, 114,
    115, 118, 127-128, 138-139, 168;
    rainbow, 77-78, 87
Tuolumne Meadows, 26, *68-69*
Tuolumne River, *4-5*
Twain, Mark, 21
Tyndall Mount, 39

U

Upper Sonoran Zone, 88, *90-93*

V

Vegetation, 56, 75-78, *79,* 82-83, *84-85,* 86-
    88, *89-103,* 146
Violet, *92*
Visalia, 23
Vole, 113

W

Wallace Creek, 29
Wallflower, *102*
Whitehead, swamp, *125*
Whitney Creek, 139
Whitney, Josiah D., *39*, 59, 60-63
Whitney, Mount, 22-25, 29, *28-29*, 33, 48-
    49, 58, 136, 140, 159, 161
Wilderness Act (1964), 26-27, 157-158,
    161, 163, 165
Windchill factor, 142
Windeler, Adolphus, 37
Winds, and effects of, 24, 102, 142
Wolverine, 144
Wolverton Creek, *143*
Woods, Lake of the, 159, 161

Y

Yarrow, 77
Yosemite Falls, 23, 45. *See also* Lower
    Yosemite Falls
Yosemite National Park, 26-27, 34, 137,
    140, 162, 166-167
Yosemite Valley, *1-2,* 22-23, 29, 59, 167-
    168, 170, *171-179*
Yuba Gap, 140